Platters and Boards

Platters and Boards

Beautiful, Casual Spreads for Every Occasion

SHELLY WESTERHAUSEN
with WYATT WORCEL

CHRONICLE BOOKS
SAN FRANCISCO

Library of Congress Cataloging-in-Publication Data

Names: Westerhausen, Shelly, author. | Worcel, Wyatt, author.
Title: Platters and boards : beautiful, casual spreads for every occasion /
   Shelly Westerhausen & Wyatt Worcel.
Description: San Francisco : Chronicle Books, [2018]
Identifiers: LCCN 2017016523 | ISBN 9781452164151 (hc : alk. paper)
Subjects: LCSH: Buffets (Cooking) | Cooking. | Entertaining. | Food
   presentation. | LCGFT: Cookbooks.
Classification: LCC TX738.5 .W47 2018 | DDC 642/.4—dc23 LC record
available at https://lccn.loc.gov/2017016523

Manufactured in China

Design by Alice Chau

Prop and food styling by Shelly Westerhausen

Oreos are a registered trademark of Intercontinental Great Brands LLC.
M&Ms are a registered trademark of Mars, Incorporated.
Nutella is a registered trademark of Ferrero S.p.A.

Chronicle books and gifts are available at special quantity discounts to
corporations, professional associations, literacy programs, and other
organizations. For details and discount information, please contact our
premiums department at corporatesales@chroniclebooks.com or at
1-800-759-0190.

10 9

Chronicle Books LLC
680 Second Street
San Francisco, California 94107
www.chroniclebooks.com

This book is dedicated to our parents:
Jan, Curt, Connie, Al, Denise & Marty

Introduction

You may have discovered your favorite cheese on the appetizer table at a sibling's wedding. Maybe your favorite night out is a drink and crudités with your best friends. Perhaps your first date was over a pot of chocolate fondue, spearing a variety of fruits and breads to drag through the dark, warm, sweet melt. Whatever your connection to boards and platters may be, this book is meant to take those special and celebratory moments of bonding over shared food into the realm of the everyday.

Have you been eyeing a beautiful walnut cutting board or a slab of slate to use as a cheese plate? This book will tell you how to make the most of all sorts of beautiful surfaces to arrange and display memorable meals and snacks. With the trend of boards taking center stage in the exploding food scene at places such as Meat & Cheese in Aspen, Colorado, Cheese & Crack Snack Shop in Portland, Oregon, and the Cheese Plate in New Paltz, New York, *Platters and Boards* is the perfect guide to help you bring these spreads into your own home.

Platters, boards, and spreads are perfect as fancy or casual starters, meals, or desserts, for a group of any size. Boards can be scaled up or down to accommodate two to two hundred hungry (or noshy) people. All the recipes in this book can easily be halved, quartered, tripled, or quadrupled to fit your needs. You'll find tips and tricks for sizing your board to fit your guest count in the first chapter.

Nothing is more versatile than a meal built on a board; it is a blank canvas for your creativity . . . or leftovers. It's a great way to use up whatever vegetables, cheeses, jams, or meats you have hanging around in your refrigerator, or use it as an opportunity to try new foods. Take a trip to that new cheese shop you've been meaning to visit or spend some time in the bulk section of your grocery store picking out an array of bulk foods worth adding to a board. It's the perfect excuse to buy a chunk of that fancy chocolate you've wanted to try or to strike up a conversation with someone at your local wine shop or winery about pairing suggestions. These artisan items elevate your creation to a conversation piece at the dinner table or your next party; people love trying new things, and boards allow them to sample a little bit of everything.

The process of putting a board together is almost as enjoyable as the noshing itself. Whether you are interested in using up what you have on hand or trying something new, take this as an opportunity to get inspired and be creative. Platters are easy to curate seasonally by featuring fruits and vegetables that are currently thriving in your area. They can also be built around a theme or the kind of items you have in your cabinet and refrigerator. Of course there are lots of ideas in this book for you, too.

Many of the boards in this book are centered around cheese, but don't let that fool you; boards and platters can be more than just cheese boards! Build your board around a central theme. That theme could be a time of year (pick produce from the spring, summer, fall, or winter), an event (a brunch gathering, a housewarming party), or even a place (a park picnic, a beach adventure). Think of it as a work of art for both the eyes and the mouth. You can pile vegetables high for a colorful, healthy tray or fill a board to the rim with candy and chocolates for a platter that appeals to the sweet tooth.

Meet the Meatless and Meat-Loving Authors

As you navigate this book, keep in mind that each board and platter has a complementary recipe, a drink pairing, and a meat suggestion from Wyatt (with the exception of the sweet boards). All the boards and recipes themselves are vegetarian with the option to add meat if you'd prefer. We did this because we wanted to be able to feed our veg- and meat-loving friends alike. The meat is additional; the boards are complete without.

As a couple with one vegetarian and one meat eater, we know firsthand how difficult it can be to create meals that satisfy both of us. We experience this in our own kitchen and at family gatherings and parties, so we are pleased that this book can bridge a gap between various diets. It is our intention that all the boards in this book are easy to size to any group, and easy to cater to many diets!

Meet the Vegetarian: Shelly

I am the meat-free, animal-loving food writer who lives for devouring freshly baked bread and wandering new farmers markets. Most of the writing and all the photography is mine, with meat suggestions contributed by Wyatt. I brought him in because I've been a vegetarian for more than fifteen years, and although I believe that meat-free meals are enough, I understand that many people want more. This is why meat is a choice in this book, an addition to make the meal more robust. As a vegetarian living with a meat eater, I've always struggled to find recipes or books that manage to accommodate both diets.

As an avid food nibbler, I often find myself craving a little of everything, so I've been known to build little spreads out of whatever I find in the refrigerator and pantry. As my collection of boards and platters began to grow, I started making bigger spreads for guests when they'd pop by for a late-afternoon cocktail or evening dinner party. I've grown to love this casual approach to serving both myself and a big crowd. It's rewarding to use up whatever I have on hand, and all the different colors and textures satisfy my love of food styling and my desire to nibble on a little bit of everything.

Meet the Meat Lover: Wyatt

I'll be your resource for all things meaty in this book. I am an underground techno artist and run a small tape label on the side, and I love to skateboard with my boxer dog, Tuko. When not working on music or hanging with my pup, I spend time helping my partner, Shelly, with food projects by hand modeling and devouring the leftover food.

On Choosing Ingredients

Most boards in this book require little or no cooking, so choosing the freshest ingredients you can get your hands on is important for the most flavorful results. We try to buy both organic and local, when possible, for our produce, cheeses, and meats.

Vegetarian Cheese

If you'd like to keep your recipes vegetarian, please note that not all cheeses are vegetarian. This is something many cooks don't realize. A good amount of cheese is made with animal rennet (enzymes derived from the stomach lining of cows, goats, sheep, and pigs) and should be avoided if you are sticking to a purely vegetarian diet. Read labels, look for a vegetarian symbol, or ask your shop's cheese expert. You may want to go even further and see if the label mentions anything about the animals being grass-fed (or organic).

This all may sound like a lot of work, but seeking out special cheeses can introduce you to an array of delicious cheeses you may have never thought to try before, and to become good friends with your shop's cheese expert in the process. For example, I tried for the longest time to find a vegetarian Brie, and the search led me to discover a slew of new favorite soft cheeses, such as triple cream, Camembert, and Vermont Creamery's Cremont, which I find to be just as satisfying and gooey.

A few of my favorite mass-produced vegetarian cheeses include Organic Valley Shredded Parmesan, BelGioioso Vegetarian Parmesan, Cypress Grove chèvre, and all of Vermont Creamery's cheeses. There are also a handful of artisan vegan cheeses that you can turn to if you are having trouble finding cruelty-free cheese. I recommend Kite Hill for upscale nut cheese options.

Because there is such a wide variety of small-batch and mass-produced cheeses all over the world, you may be able to find a type of vegetarian cheese in one region and not another. If you are having trouble finding a certain kind of cheese to fit your dietary needs, check to see what category it falls in (see cheese types on page 18) and substitute another cheese in the same group that fits your needs.

Properly Sourced Meats

We eat a lot of vegetarian meals since I do most of the cooking in our house, but Wyatt can't resist a meal based on meat now and then. It is important to purchase free-range, grass-fed meat if possible, sourced from local farmers. Generally speaking, locally sourced meat simply tastes better (in Wyatt's opinion). It is usually leaner and contains more nutrients. It is better for the environment because it's not shipped from far away or raised in an intensive feedlot, so it reduces the use of fossil fuels, and the animals are usually treated better. Lastly, you are supporting the local economy and the wonderful community you live in.

How to Create the Perfect Board or Platter

Here are the basic concepts that go into creating your own board or platter with whatever you have on hand, at any time. A cheese plate is probably the first thing that comes to mind, but there are boards of all kinds: antipasto platters, veggie trays, holiday cookie samplers, relish trays, and charcuterie boards, to name a few. These well-known boards and platters are great ideas to start with—and spin off from—when building your own.

I mention cheese boards frequently in this section; as they're so well known and ubiquitous, there's plenty of etiquette already. But this information applies to all kinds of boards. Here are a few terms to keep in mind when reading this chapter.

Boards, platters, and trays: I use these terms interchangeably to describe the surface you arrange the food on. This could be anything from a ceramic plate to a cutting board, slate slab, or antique metal tray.

Spreads: We consider a spread to be a grouping of platters or boards that all have food built around a central theme. You'll see a number of these arrangements in this book.

Picking a Board, Platter, or Tray

Selecting the serving surface for your grouping of foods will help determine how much space you have to work with. Be sure to pick something large enough so the food isn't crowded (and hard to pick up). Choose a neutral-colored surface (such as white, black, gray, or beige) to help the food pop and not distract from your theme. Don't be afraid to play around with different shapes or surfaces, or to mix and match a few to create a buffet-style vibe.

The following materials all make great platters and boards.

Wood: Use a big cutting board or cheeseboard made out of wood. This is probably the most accessible material, and the options are vast with boards in all sorts of shapes and types of woods, at all price points. A good-looking wooden board is a terrific gift (for you or from you), and can be found in a variety of price points and designs. If using food that is dark, a lighter wood (such as oak, maple, or cherry) might work best to let the colors pop. On the flip side, use a dark wood (such as olive or walnut) to feature light-colored food.

Pick out a nonporous wood (such as olive wood, birch, or hard maple), as it will not absorb liquids or strong flavors as easily. Make sure you choose a wood with a food-safe finish (it's safest to stick to boards found in the cooking section of stores or those labeled specifically for food use). Clean it with warm soap and water after each use and wipe dry immediately. You can also purchase food-friendly wood cleaners.

Marble, granite, and other stone: Achieve a classic look with a marble pastry slab or granite cheeseboard. Stone is also great for keeping your food cool, as it's naturally dense and doesn't conduct heat very well (keep this in mind if you're putting out a platter on a warm day!). A downside to keep in mind is that these types of boards will be relatively heavy compared to many other surface options.

Another downside of using marble, in particular, is that it does stain easily, so you'll want to make sure any sort of vibrant vegetable (like beets) doesn't rest on it for long periods of time. Make sure to find a food-safe marble cleaner for your board, as it will absorb odors over time.

Metal trays: Metal trays are generally very light and are easy to find at your local cookware store or antique shop. They can also be found in both light and dark colors and are easy to clean.

Slate or chalkboard: A dark slate or chalkboard surface provides a nice color contrast to food, giving it an appealing visual pop. It is also nonporous, which prevents it from absorbing and melding flavors on the board. You can use chalk on it to illustrate or write out what is being served. One drawback: It does scratch easily, so you may begin to see scuffs after a few uses.

Pink salt: A strikingly beautiful pink Himalayan salt slab makes a wonderful platter. Use this whenever you'd like to add a pop of pink and a hint of salt to your food, such as the Build Your Own Crostini Spread (page 90).

Ceramic: Ceramic platters come in all shapes, colors, and sizes. Find an heirloom antique in your parents' basement or purchase one from your favorite homewares store. For the purposes of this book, keep the shape basic (oval, circle, or square) and the color neutral (white, black, tan, or gray) so as to not distract from the food. Another option might be to get several ceramic platters that are similar, arrange them on the table, and assemble the food across them all.

Once you pick your serving surface, don't forget all the other necessary tools such as knives, forks, mini spoons, wooden picks, and labels (if serving cheese or anything of special note). Read on to learn more about the additional props you'll need.

Props for Your Board

These are the complementary supplies that will also be on the board. Here are a few things to make sure you have handy when assembling the board:

Tongs: Consider putting out mini tongs for guests to easily pick up the food without getting their hands all over the rest of the food on the platter. This could be especially important if you are working with a platter that is loaded to the brim.

Cheese knives and forks: Place small knives and forks (often sold as "cheese knives" and "cheese forks") near the cheese for easy serving. Depending on what kind of cheese you are serving, you may want to provide a different knife for every cheese so that the flavors don't mix together while slicing.

Wooden picks: Providing wooden picks alongside a board allows guests to pick up fruit pieces or other small or sticky morsels without getting them on their hands. Use anything from basic toothpicks to elaborate skewers.

Cheese labels: These are useful when you are serving unusual cheeses that your guests might not be familiar with, or to inform any guests who may have dietary concerns or restrictions. They come in a variety of shapes and sizes, but the most common are flags or ceramic sticks that usually have a chalkboard space to write on.

Vessels (small bowls or plates): Spills aren't pretty, so make sure you have fashionable vessels handy for containing jams, honey, and anything else that could bleed all over the setup. A variety of wooden, glass, or metal bowls, mini Mason jars, and shallow ceramic dishes or ramekins will come in handy.

Linens/napkins: If you're having a formal gathering, make sure to bring out the linens to keep guests from getting food on their nice clothes. For casual gatherings, most boards have finger foods, so having napkins nearby for guests to use as plates and wipe their hands with is essential.

Parchment paper: If you are worried about food seeping into your board or platter or are looking for an easy cleanup, place a sheet of parchment paper over your surface before assembling.

Assembling a Board or Platter

By far the best part about making a board or platter is getting creative with all the ingredients you have on hand. Don't be afraid to experiment! The following section walks you through the components of different boards and platters, so you will have the tools to create your own boards and stray as far from the recipes as you'd like.

Here is a loose order of operations on how to assemble your board, along with lots of little tips to keep in mind when planning your spread:

1. Choose your surface. We talked about a wide range of surface options in the previous section (page 12), so figure out which one will be the star of the show this time around. Don't be afraid to use more than one surface if you need it. This is especially true when you are mixing sweet and savory foods. It can be just as stunning to have a whole table full of plates brimming with food as it is to have just one large board.

2. Invent your theme. This can involve picking one of the many boards I've outlined in this book or coming up with your own based on the season, an occasion, or even a color scheme.

3. Find the main food or foods to base your board around. The options are endless when it comes to what you can put on a board, so I recommend picking

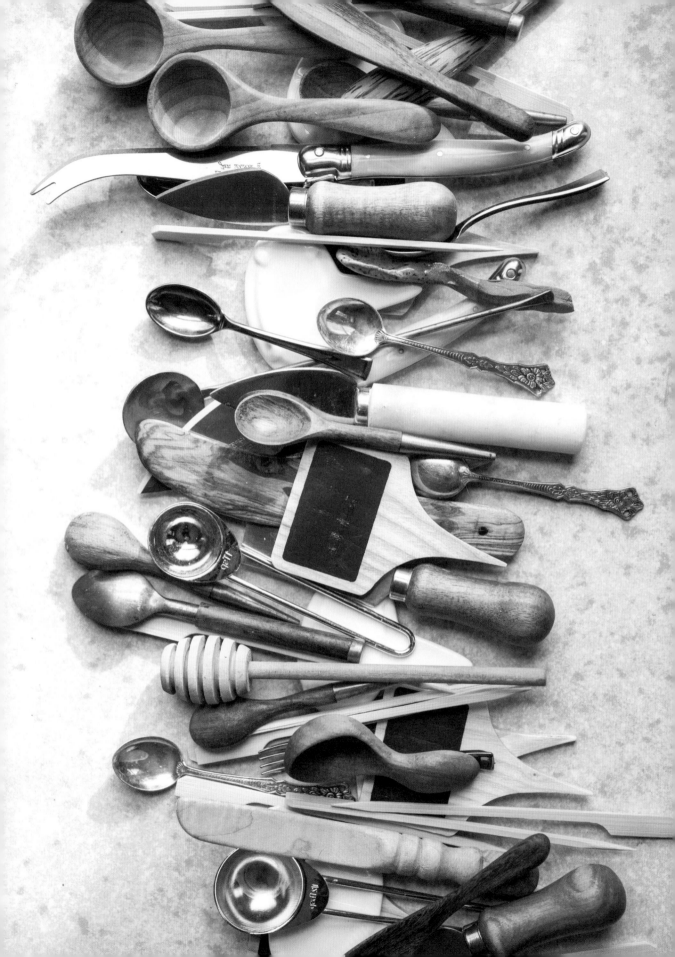

an item or two you for sure want to serve. If cheeses are the main component of your board, arrange these first and then place everything else around them. This will ensure that there's adequate space around the cheeses so they don't accidently absorb each other's flavors. When serving cheese, remove the wrapping or packaging but keep the rinds on.

4. Determine what your complementary items are. Once you've picked the main food for your board, choose an array of complementary foods to serve alongside and fill out the board with. Make sure you are getting a little bit of salty, sweet, savory, and tangy on your board (unless, of course, it's an all-sweets board).

5. Start spare, and add food components one at a time, working outward from the main item. Some boards look great piled high with as much food as you can fit in an area, while others will look overwhelmingly cluttered. Start with your main food items and then add components, one at a time, until the board looks good to you. When working with cheeses, I prefer to place them on different parts of the boards, to avoid the flavors mixing, and then fill the complementary items in around them. Another option may be to cluster certain food items into their own areas of the boards. For example, for the Breakfast Sandwich Table Spread on page 38, it may make sense to put all the bread options in one area and the garnish options in another.

6. Add any additional tools such as utensils, labels, and food picks. Add serving spoons and knives for each cheese and dip so that the food doesn't mix while guests are serving themselves. This is also a good time to check to see if any of the foods you are working with might seep or spread. If so, place them in their own small dishes to prevent them from flavoring or running into your other foods.

7. Voilà! It's time to serve and eat your creation! Generally, you'll want to assemble the board where you'll be serving it to avoid ruining the presentation you worked so meticulously to create. Make sure to start putting your board together at least an hour before guests arrive (so the cheese can come to room temperature), adding any meat components 15 minutes before, and any items that may wilt or melt (such as fresh herbs, edible flowers, or ice cream) 5 minutes before.

I touched on this a bit already but wanted to mention it again since it is one of the biggest mistakes I see over and over when people first start making their own boards: You might be tempted to leave your platter or board uncrowded and sparse, perhaps to prevent flavors from mixing, to allow components to stand out on their own, and to create a final product that looks put-together and clean. Although there is a time and place for that approach, more often than not I like to stack a huge amount of food onto a board. It guarantees I don't have to keep refilling it all night. Also, a board brimming with different textures and shapes creates a huge, appealing presentation. It's generous. If you aren't sure if you are going for simple and put-together or overflowing and brimming, start sparse and slowly add more food until it looks good to you.

Savory Boards and Platters

Savory boards are the most common and offer the greatest opportunity for variety. Here I'll run through the different types of cheeses mentioned throughout this book so you can easily reference this section when swapping cheeses on your boards. First and foremost, make sure you are getting an array of textures and flavors on your board; you'll want a mix of tangy, savory, salty, crunchy, and even a hint of sweet. Make sure you are adding more to your boards than just cheese. A variety of foods allows your guests to cleanse their palates between cheese bites and appeals to a broader range of people.

Here is a list of suggestions for what to include on a savory board. When creating your own board, try including a mix of most of the following ideas to create a well-rounded platter:

Cheese (Savory/Salty)

Let's start with the obvious: Cheese is a classic when it comes to creating boards. It can easily be the center of attention and the thing to build your board around. Stick to two to four cheeses for your board, to present enough variety to interest but not overwhelm your guests. You may also want to consider having at least one familiar cheese (such as Cheddar, Swiss, Muenster, etc.) for nonadventurous guests. Here are the different types of cheeses to choose from:

Firm and hard: Firm cheeses are perhaps the most well-known of all the categories. The majority of the whey is removed before the cheese is cooked, giving it the firm texture that makes it easy to slice. Serve hard cheeses either in portioned-out slices or in one big wedge. They pair well with buttery crackers and juicy fruit such as apples. Examples of hard cheeses include Cheddar, Asiago, Manchego, Percorino Romano, provolone, and Parmigiano.

Semisoft: With medium moisture levels, semisoft cheese comes in two varieties: interior-ripened and surface-ripened. For interior-ripened cheese, the aging process starts from the center and ends at the exterior. For surface-ripened, the aging process starts at the exterior. Semisoft cheeses pair well with dark breads (such as rye or pumpernickel) and savory nuts like almonds and walnuts. Serve in wedges or plate entire wheels with individual knives for each kind. Examples of this type of cheese include Havarti, Gouda, Monterey Jack, fontina, and Muenster.

Soft: Soft cheeses have medium moisture levels with interiors that have not been pressed or cooked, yielding a creamy texture. Serve these cheeses in wedges, or present the entire wheel with knives alongside. Soft cheeses pair beautifully with wheat crackers and sweet or juicy components such as pears or fig jam. In some cases, particularly oozy cheeses may even need to be contained in their own bowls or plates. Examples of this type of cheese include Brie, queso fresco, feta, and panela.

Fresh: Fresh cheese is made by the simple process of leaving milk out to curdle. The moisture level is usually high in this type of cheese. Fresh cheeses also tend to go bad more quickly than other forms of cheese, which is something to keep in mind when buying ahead of your event. Serve these cheeses in small bowls or shallow dishes with a serving spoon or

knife. Fresh cheese pairs wonderfully with a soft baguette or fruit jam. You will find some crossover among fresh and soft cheeses; for example, mozzarella and Burrata are often referred to as both fresh and soft cheeses. Other examples of these cheeses are ricotta, mascarpone, cottage cheese, cream cheese, and crème fraîche.

Blue-veined: Blue-veined cheese has certain cultures incorporated into it to promote the growth of a bluish-green mold. Since that is usually rather pungent, use this cheese sparingly as a little goes a long way. It pairs nicely with sweet components like fruit and honey. Serve either crumbled or in wedges. Examples of this type of cheese include Gorgonzola, blue Stilton, Danish blue, and Roquefort.

Use this cheese list to swap around cheeses throughout the book. If a recipe calls for a soft cheese you aren't excited about or can't find, reference this list when figuring out a substitute for it. Try to include a few different cheese categories in each board.

Bread and Crackers (Salty/Savory)

Guests will need a vehicle to get spreads and toppings from the plate to their mouths, which is where bases like crackers, slices of bread, bagel chips, pita slices, and crisps come in. Consider keeping it simple when it comes to the flavors of your crackers and bread as to not overshadow whatever your toppings may be. Also, consider using one soft and one hard base (such as hard crackers and a soft baguette) to give your guests a variety.

Pickled and Marinated Food (Tangy)

These foods act as palate cleansers between bites and even help heighten the flavor of some foods. Olives are a standard go-to here, but marinated artichoke hearts and pickled vegetables (green beans, beets, peppers, carrots) are also great choices, especially for adding pops of color and different shapes and textures to your board.

Fruit (Sweet)

Dried fruit is great because it can easily be precut and portioned out into bite-size pieces. Grapes and fresh figs are also an easy addition for boards.

Sweet Bites (Sweet)

If you'd like something sweet on your board other than fruit, consider adding pieces of quality chocolate or candied nuts.

Spreads & Condiments (Sweet/Savory/Tangy)

There are a ton of artisanal condiments out there to jazz up your board. It's fun to discover new varieties of spicy mustard, sweet jams, tapenade, honey, chutney, and other spreads. Premade condiments are a fuss-free and easy addition to your platter.

Nuts or Cured Meat (Savory/Salty)

Add some substantial protein components for a filling addition. Think salty nuts or cured meats that can be left out for long periods of time without spoiling.

Garnish

If your final presentation feels lacking at all, consider adding fresh herbs, edible flowers, or seasonal greens for brightness and color.

I know that was a ton of information to process in order to create your own board. There are obviously lots of exceptions to these when it comes to creating very specific boards like vegetable platters and antipasto plates. However, if you are looking to create a general board, this list is a great starting point. If you need a little more guidance, I suggest you check out the Clean Out Your Pantry Smorgasbord on page 194 to see these items in action.

Sweet Boards and Platters

For sweet platters, try to group everything by category. For example, cluster all the chocolate items together, put candies in another area, and group cookies and other miscellaneous sweets somewhere else. Also, if something has the potential to melt over time, make sure to put it on a separate tray so it doesn't seep into the other items.

Keep the same concepts in mind when making your sweet board: Try to pick out food that has a variety of textures, colors, and shapes so the end result is stunning and unique.

Spreads

In addition to boards and platters, you'll come across several recipes labeled as "spreads" in this book. Spreads will be an entire table filled with plates, platters, and boards full of food. They are less about fitting everything onto one platter and more about filling the entire table with edible bites, arranged around a theme. I like to use the term "spread" when talking about many of the "build your own" boards in this book, since the ingredients are laid out over several plates and trays. Make sure to use similar surfaces throughout the table to keep a cohesive feeling. Also,

you'll want to keep the same concepts in mind for spreads when it comes to picking out a variety of flavors, textures, and colors for the food.

Portioning Your Board for One to One Hundred people

I wish that I could have a hotline number for you to call every week before you put on a party. You could call me up and say, "Shelly, I *love* this board on page X and want to make it for my party next week. The only problem I have is that it serves XXX and I have twenty people coming. What do I do?" I'd pull out my portioning grid and start doing all the math right there while on the phone with you. We'd then talk it out and move on to discussing the decorations and playlist.

Unfortunately, this hotline idea is a logistical nightmare, so instead I am going to share my "mysterious" portioning grid with you. Portioning is never going to be an exact science since store-bought ingredients are available in different quantities and sizes, but it should get you close enough. If you are nervous at all about how much to buy, I always lean on the side of purchasing too much, just in case. I'd much rather be eating leftover cheese and crackers for a few days than to run out halfway through my event.

Here are the serving suggestions for a few of the main foods you'll find in this book (note that these are assuming each will be served with a variety of other components):

Cheese

Starter / After Dinner:
 1 oz per person
Main: 1 to 2 oz per person

Nuts

Starter / After Dinner:
 1 to 2 Tbsp per person
Main: 2 to 3 Tbsp per person

Condiments

Starter / After Dinner:
 1 to 2 Tbsp per person
Main: 3 to 4 Tbsp per person

Fruit

Starter / After Dinner:
 4 pieces per person
Main: 4 to 5 pieces per person

Vegetables

Starter / After Dinner:
 4 to 6 pieces per person
Main: 6 to 10 pieces per person

Cookies

Starter / After Dinner:
 2 cookies per person

Chips

Starter / After Dinner:
 1 oz per person
Main: 1 oz per person

Meat

Starter / After Dinner:
 1 to 2 oz per person
Main: 2 to 3 oz per person

A Few Notes on Serving and Storing

Traditionally, you'll want to serve savory boards before dinner and sweet boards after. There are a few boards in this book that have both savory and sweet components, and those can be served anytime.

Always take the cheese out of the refrigerator at least 1 hour and up to 2 hours before serving. Cheese reaches its optimal flavor and texture at room temperature, and some of the more complex flavors of the cheese won't shine through if chilled when serving.

If serving meat with your board, remove it from the refrigerator 15 to 20 minutes before serving.

Because of these guidelines, I advise that you start to put the board together an hour before your guests arrive. Then just add anything that needs to be chilled or warm when you add the meat, 15 minutes before guests arrive. This will ensure not only that the food is at optimal flavor but also that you're ready to go when guests start arriving.

As for storing any leftover cheese and meat, wrap it in parchment, wax, or cheese paper and place in individual resealable plastic bags. Condiments can be transferred to sealable jars and vegetables and nuts into resealable bags. Store everything in the refrigerator.

A Board for Every Occasion

Have an event, holiday, meal, or party coming up and not sure what board to make for it? Use the following list to help you figure out what to make!

Housewarming Party

Holiday Parties

Game Night or Book Club

Bridal Shower

Part One:

Morn

ing

Lazy Sunday Brunch BOARD

With almost as little effort as it takes to make eggs and toast, this board is the ideal lazy spread when you don't want to change out of your pajamas.

STRATEGY: Use the ciabatta soldiers for both the eggs and cheese. You can eat them separately but I prefer to add both a piece of cheese and a piece of runny egg onto the bread for an open-face sandwich vibe.

DRINK PAIRING: Serve with lattes! If you don't have a machine at home, have someone run out and grab a few lattes while you are cooking up the soft-boiled eggs.

WYATT'S MEATY SUGGESTION: Add a link of Spanish chorizo. Unlike fresh Mexican chorizo that must be cooked, this spicy Spanish sausage is the perfect lazy breakfast fare because it is ready to eat upon purchasing.

SERVES 4

8 oz [230 g] Gruyère cheese

4 oz [115 g] fresh goat cheese

1 cup [125 g] Granola Two Ways (page 49) or store-bought granola or cereal

2 large tomatoes, sliced and sprinkled with salt, or 1 bunch small vine tomatoes

2 cups [240 g] sliced fresh fruit

Soft-Boiled Eggs with Savory Parmesan Soldiers (recipe follows)

Place the cheeses, granola, tomato slices, and fresh fruit all on their own individual small plates or bowls and arrange on a board. Add serving spoons and small knives to the plates and bowls. Fill the remaining space with eggs in their egg cups and Parmesan soldiers. Serve right away.

Soft-Boiled Eggs
with Savory
Parmesan Soldiers

Soft-Boiled Eggs with Savory Parmesan Soldiers

SERVES 4 AS A BOARD COMPONENT

- **8 oz [230 g] ciabatta loaf**
- **1 Tbsp unsalted butter, at room temperature**
- **¼ cup [20 g] grated Parmesan cheese**
- **Dash of freshly ground black pepper**
- **4 eggs**

Place a rack in the upper third of the oven and preheat to 400°F [200°C].

Place your hand on top of the ciabatta loaf and carefully cut all the way through the side of the ciabatta loaf to make two even pieces. Cut each half into 8 strips crosswise for a total of 16 strips. Spread half the butter onto the crust sides and transfer to a baking sheet, crust-side up. Bake for 3 minutes, flip, and spread the other side with the remaining butter, the Parmesan, and a dash of pepper. Return to the oven and bake until browned and crispy on top, about 6 minutes.

Meanwhile, bring a small saucepan of water to a boil over medium-high heat. Once at a rapid boil, reduce the heat to a rapid simmer and carefully add the whole eggs. Simmer for 5 to 7 minutes (7 if you like your whites completely cooked). Drain and run under cold water for 30 seconds.

Place the eggs, pointy side down, in egg cups and carefully use a knife to crack the egg shell in a horizontal movement all the way around the egg (about one-third from the top). Once the egg shell is cracked all the way around, gently push the knife all the way through the egg and remove the top part of the egg and shell to serve on the side. Enjoy right away by dipping the Parmesan soldiers into the egg yolks.

Caffeine SPREAD

These scones are too good not to build an entire spread around them. This is perfect for the coffee-obsessed person in your life or to give your guests an extra jolt of morning energy.

STRATEGY: This spread brings home-made coffee bars to the next level. Make your iced coffee and espresso at the very last step so they are fresh and center stage.

DRINK PAIRING: You'll be enjoying iced coffee and espresso. Make it a part of the spread so that it feels like a fancy morning coffee station with scones, chocolate, and all the coffee mix-ins.

WYATT'S MEATY SUGGESTION: Try serving this with cured sausage. Bonus points if you can find one cured with coffee!

SERVES 8

6 oz [170 g] chocolate-covered coffee beans

Cardamom Coffee Cream Scones (recipe follows)

10 to 12 sugar cubes

4 Tbsp [55 g] salted butter, at room temperature

1-in [2.5-cm] piece honeycomb or ¼ cup [85 g] honey

¼ cup [60 ml] heavy cream

8 cups [2 L] iced coffee

8 espresso shots

Transfer the chocolate-covered coffee beans to a small bowl and place on a serving board. Add the scones, sugar cubes, butter, and honeycomb to the serving board, keeping everything spread far enough apart that it doesn't touch (to avoid flavors mingling). Pour heavy cream into a pitcher and add to the board. Pour iced coffee into a pitcher or individual glasses (depending on how you'd like to serve it) and espresso shots into espresso glasses. Place around or near the board encouraging people to dress their coffee with cream and sugar cubes and try the scones topped with butter and honey. Serve right away.

Cardamom
Coffee Cream
Scones

Cardamom Coffee Cream Scones

MAKES 8 SCONES

½ cup [120 ml] heavy cream +
  more for brushing on scones

1 egg

1 egg yolk

1 tsp vanilla extract

2¼ cups [270 g] all-purpose flour

¼ cup [50 g] sugar

1 Tbsp baking powder

2 tsp ground coffee

1 tsp ground cardamom

½ tsp fine sea salt

½ cup [110 g] cold unsalted butter,
  cut into pieces

Coarse sugar, for sprinkling

Line a baking sheet with parchment paper and set aside.

In a small bowl, whisk together the cream, egg, egg yolk, and vanilla. In a medium mixing bowl, whisk together the flour, sugar, baking powder, coffee, cardamom, and salt. Add the butter to the flour mixture and use a pastry blender or a fork to work it into a coarse meal. Add the egg mixture and mix with a fork until the dough barely comes together (be careful not to overmix, or your scones will be tough).

Turn the dough out onto a clean surface and knead three or four times, or just until the dough comes together. Press the dough into a 6-in [15-cm] disc and cut into eight equal triangles. Transfer to the prepared baking sheet and place in the freezer for 30 minutes.

Preheat the oven to 400°F [200°C].

Brush the tops of the scones with cream and sprinkle with coarse sugar. Bake until brown on top, 17 to 20 minutes. Transfer to a wire rack to cool until the scones can be handled. Serve warm.

To store, transfer scones to an airtight container. They can be stored at room temperature for up to 24 hours but are best enjoyed the day they are baked.

Breakfast

Sando

Tab

Ricotta and Tomato Baked Eggs

Breakfast Sandwich Table

SPREAD

Having a brunch gathering? Prepare this collection of fixings that allows your guests to customize their sandwiches.

 STRATEGY: You have two options for presentation here: You can make an assembly-line table off to the side for guests to gravitate to when they are hungry, or you can set up a big spread on your dining-room table if you are planning for everyone to sit down at once to eat. If going the assembly-line route, buy presliced cheese and make sure to slice the bagels, croissants, and ciabatta beforehand to keep your guest line moving. Cluster ingredients onto several trays or boards based on these groupings: breads, toppings and cheeses, and spreads and garnishes.

If you have the dining space, I'd recommend going the family-style route with a large sit-down brunch spread. This centers the morning on the food and gives the gathering a formal vibe. If guests offer to bring a dish, home fries and a fruit salad would pair beautifully with this spread.

DRINK PAIRING: You are making a huge spread for your guests, so if anyone offers to bring drinks, suggest Bloody Mary supplies and put them in charge of whipping them up when they arrive.

 WYATT'S MEATY SUGGESTION: Nothing gets me out of bed faster than the smell of bacon frying in a pan. Bacon is sure to add an addictive, greasy crunch to these breakfast sandwiches.

SERVES 12

4 bagels, sliced

4 croissants, sliced

4 slices ciabatta bread

12 tomato slices (from about 3 large tomatoes)

2½ cups [50 g] arugula

Ricotta and Tomato Baked Eggs (recipe follows)

2 bell peppers, cut into strips

4 Swiss cheese slices

4 pepper Jack cheese slices

4 Cheddar cheese slices

½ cup [125 g] Pistachio Herb Pesto (page 210) or store-bought pesto

6 Tbsp [90 g] Whole-Grain Ale Mustard (page 209) or store-bought whole-grain mustard

½ cup [150 g] Tomato-Thyme Jam (page 113) or store-bought savory jam (such as red pepper jelly)

1 bunch fresh basil

12 oz [330 g] Bread and Butter Pickled Vegetables (page 187) or store-bought pickles

36 pitted olives

Fine sea salt

Freshly ground black pepper

For an assembly line setting: Place serving plates and utensils for the guests to use on the far left of the table. Place the bagels, croissants, and ciabatta on the first tray (the one that is farthest to the left). Place the tomato slices on a rimmed dish (to keep the juices from spreading) and add to a second tray along with the arugula, baked eggs, bell peppers, and cheeses. Place the tongs near the cheese along with any spoons or forks that will be needed to easily pick up the vegetables. Place the pesto, mustard, and jam in three small bowls. Place the pesto bowl, mustard bowl, jam bowl, basil, pickled vegetables, olives, salt well, and pepper grinder on the last tray, along with serving spoons for each one, and put it to the far right of the table.

As soon as it's all ready and set up, call your guests to the assembly line. Make sure they come and enjoy it while it's hot!

Alternatively, if you are planning to host a sit-down brunch, set the table for twelve with plates and utensils. Transfer all of the food into individual bowls and/or serving dishes and place out on the table. Make sure to have enough serving spoons and forks on the table as well for dishing the food out. Serve as soon as it's ready and set up.

Ricotta and Tomato Baked Eggs

SERVES 12 AS A BOARD COMPONENT

8 eggs

1¼ cups [300 ml] whole milk

1 tsp fine sea salt

1 tsp dried oregano

Dash of freshly ground black pepper

8 oz [230 g] whole-milk ricotta

15 cherry tomatoes

1 heaping Tbsp shredded Parmesan cheese

Preheat the oven to 375°F [190°C] and grease a 9-by-13-in [23-by-33-cm] rectangle pan.

Whisk together the eggs, milk, salt, oregano, and pepper. Pour the mixture into the prepared pan. Spoon heaping spoonfuls of ricotta into the egg mixture, placing them as evenly as possible throughout the eggs. Sprinkle in the tomatoes, filling any spaces between dollops of ricotta. Sprinkle the top with Parmesan and bake until the eggs are completely set and starting to brown, about 30 to 40 minutes.

Remove from the oven and season with salt and pepper. Let cool for 10 minutes and then serve warm.

Roasted Figs
with Tarragon

unch

for a Crowd

Brunch for a Crowd

BOARD

Impress your guests with more than just a bag of bagels or a box of donuts! This board tantalizes with an array of delicious brunch foods perfect for feeding a crowd.

STRATEGY: I'd recommend piling your board high with as much food as you can fit, for a stunning presentation, and to save you from constantly refilling it during the party! This spread serves a lot, so don't hesitate to split it into several boards if you don't have a serving board large enough. Top sliced bread with roasted figs and Burrata cheese for the ultimate crostini!

DRINK PAIRING: Pull out that bottle of champagne and a jug of orange juice and whip up a batch of mimosas. It doesn't get easier, and if you are anything like me, you were probably already looking for an excuse to drink champagne at breakfast.

WYATT'S MEATY SUGGESTION: Instead of turning to the famous breakfast meat, bacon, try out prosciutto as a perfect pairing to go with the roasted figs and soft cheese.

SERVES 12

6 oz [170 g] soft cheese (such as Camembert or mozzarella)

Roasted Figs with Tarragon (recipe follows)

8 oz [230 g] Burrata cheese

3 cups [400 g] marinated olives

12 hard-boiled eggs

¾ cup [255 g] honey or 3-in [7.5-cm] piece honeycomb

24 baguette or ciabatta slices

8 oz [230 g] crackers or breadsticks

8 oz [230 g] sesame sticks

3 cups [480 g] seedless red grapes

3 cups [370 g] Granola Two Ways (page 49) or store-bought granola

3 cups [420 g] mixed nuts

Place the soft cheese on a small-rimmed dish and add to the center of the board along with a serving knife. Add the roasted figs, Burrata, olives, hard-boiled eggs, and honey to individual bowls, along with small serving spoons, and space evenly across the board. Fill in any spaces with piles of bread slices, crackers or breadsticks, sesame sticks, grapes, granola, and mixed nuts.

Roasted Figs with Tarragon

MAKES 12 FIG HALVES

1 Tbsp unsalted butter

¼ cup [85 g] honey

Pinch of fine sea salt

1 sprig fresh tarragon +
more for serving

6 Mission figs, halved

Preheat the oven to 400°F [200°C].

Place the butter in a small baking dish and place it in the oven to melt while it preheats. Once the butter is melted, carefully remove the baking dish from the oven and whisk the honey and salt into the butter to create a thick sauce. Add the tarragon sprig and gently press it down so that it's completely covered in the sauce. Add the figs, cut-side down, in a single layer and spoon the sauce over the figs so they are completely coated. Transfer to the oven and bake for 10 to 12 minutes, or until very soft.

Remove from the oven, garnish with additional tarragon, and serve warm.

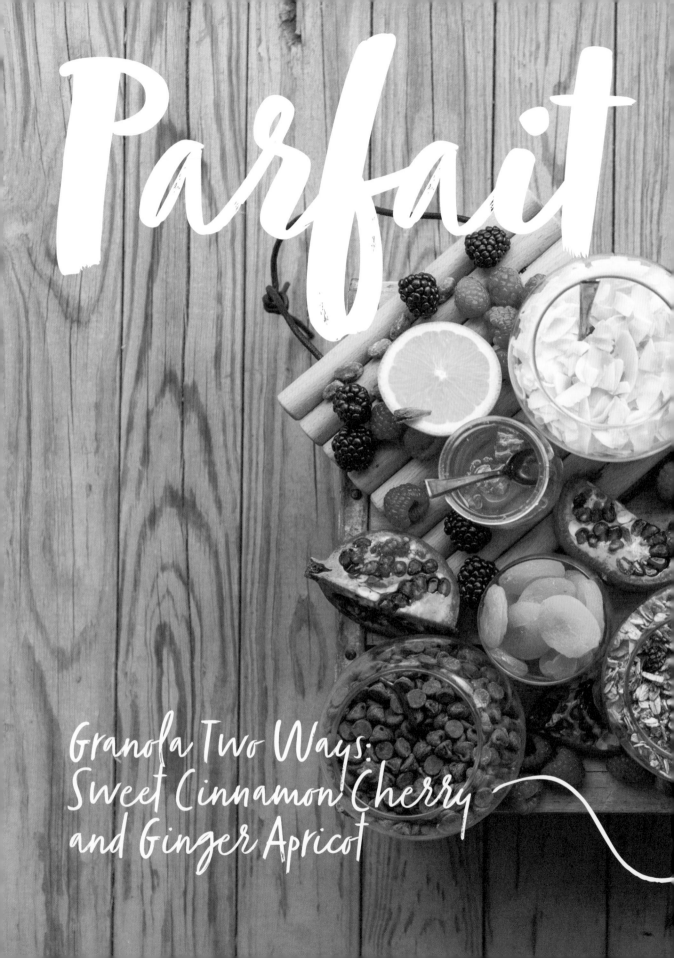

Parfait

Granola Two Ways: Sweet Cinnamon Cherry and Ginger Apricot

Parfait BOARD

This board is your best bet when you have to feed a crowd first thing in the morning but don't want to wake up early to cook.

STRATEGY : Prepare the granola the evening before. Set out all the toppings before your guests arrive and then set the yogurt out right before serving.

DRINK PAIRING: Serve a few of your favorite fruit juices. This could be as simple as buying your favorite premade juices or as labor-intensive as spending some time juicing before your meal—your choice!

WYATT'S MEATY SUGGESTION: Serve with a side of breakfast sausage links for a savory contrast to your sweet and light parfait.

SERVES 8

8 cups [2 L] plain yogurt

Sweet Cinnamon Cherry Granola or Ginger Apricot Granola (recipes follow)

1½ cups [180 g] chopped shelled pistachios

½ cup [60 g] chopped almonds

1½ cups [210 g] fresh berries

½ cup [80 g] dried apricot pieces

½ cup [40 g] coconut flakes

¼ cup [55 g] dried fruit (such as apricots, blueberries, raisins, etc.)

½ cup [60 g] semisweet chocolate chips

½ cup [120 ml] maple syrup

½ cup [170 g] honey

1 cup [12 g] packed fresh mint leaves

Place all the ingredients in individual bowls. Starting with the side where your guests will begin, place bowls, spoons, and yogurt followed by the bowls of nuts, chopped fruit, chocolate chips, syrup, honey, and ending with the mint garnish. Add serving spoons to each bowl.

Granola Two Ways: Sweet Cinnamon Cherry and Ginger Apricot

SERVES 8 AS A BOARD COMPONENT

Sweet Cinnamon Cherry Granola:

2 cups [160 g] old-fashioned rolled oats

½ cup [40 g] coconut flakes

½ cup [55 g] chopped pecans

2 tsp ground cinnamon

Pinch of fine sea salt

¼ cup [85 g] honey

¼ cup [60 ml] sunflower seed oil

1 egg white, whisked until frothy

¼ cup [35 g] dried cherries

Ginger Apricot Granola:

2 cups [160 g] old-fashioned rolled oats

½ cup [40 g] coconut flakes

½ cup [55 g] chopped pecans

2 tsp ground ginger

Pinch of fine sea salt

¼ cup [85 g] honey

¼ cup [60 ml] sunflower seed oil

1 egg white, whisked until frothy

¼ cup [40 g] chopped apricots

Preheat the oven to 300°F [150°C] and line a large baking sheet with parchment paper.

In a medium mixing bowl, combine the oats, coconut flakes, pecans, cinnamon (for the Sweet Cinnamon Cherry Granola) or ginger (for the Ginger Apricot Granola), and salt. Fold in the honey and oil until completely coated. Fold in the egg white. Transfer to the prepared baking sheet and spread out into an even layer.

Bake for 30 to 35 minutes, stirring every 15 minutes, or until golden brown.

Remove from the oven and fold in the dried cherries or apricots. Let cool completely before serving. Store in an airtight container at room temperature for up to 2 weeks.

Breakfast Rolls

Wa

nderlust

Wanderlust BOARD

I wish I could include all my favorite foods from traveling the world, but there was no way to make a board big enough! So I focused on favorites from my European adventures—I loved our breakfasts in Germany with fresh-baked breakfast rolls served with jams, cheeses, butter, and cold cuts. There are also bits of France (croissants!) and Ireland (Irish tea!).

STRATEGY: Prep the rolls all the way up to their second proofing the night before so they'll be baked fresh in the morning and you won't have to wake up at the crack of dawn.

DRINK PAIRING: Serve this with Irish breakfast tea and shots of espresso. Take a tally of who wants tea and who wants espresso so you can prep just the right amount when serving.

WYATT'S MEATY SUGGESTION: Top the warm rolls with cold cuts, butter, cheese, and mustard.

SERVES 8

- 4 oz [115 g] sliceable foreign cheese (such as Parmesan, Fiore Sardo, Cheddar, etc.)
- 4 oz [115 g] soft or spreadable foreign cheese (such as chèvre, blue Stilton, etc.)
- 1 small loaf pumpernickel bread, sliced and toasted
- 8 small fresh croissants, biscotti, or a mixture of both
- ¼ cup [75 g] elderberry or lingonberry jam
- ½ cup [65 g] olives
- ¼ cup [70 g] Nutella hazelnut spread
- 4 Tbsp [55 g] European-style butter
- 4 cups [960 g] plain yogurt
- ¼ cup [60 g] Whole-Grain Ale Mustard (page 209) or store-bought whole-grain mustard
- 2 cups [280 g] chopped fruit
- Breakfast Rolls (recipe follows)

Plate the cheeses, making sure to leave enough room so they do not touch. Add the cheese plate to a serving tray. Place all the other ingredients onto small-rimmed serving plates or into bowls and arrange on the serving tray. Add serving knives and spoons to each individual plate or bowl. Serve right away.

Breakfast Rolls

MAKES 8 ROLLS

- 2¼ tsp active dry yeast
- 1 tsp sugar
- ⅔ cup [160 ml] warm water (110°F / 43°C)
- ½ cup + 1 Tbsp [135 ml] whole milk
- 1 tsp fine sea salt
- 4 cups [480 g] all-purpose flour
- Olive oil, for greasing the bowl
- Ice cubes

Line a baking sheet with parchment paper.

Place the yeast, sugar, and warm water in the bowl of a stand mixer fitted with a paddle attachment. Let sit until the yeast is frothy, 5 to 7 minutes. Add ½ cup [120 ml] of the milk and the salt. Turn the mixer on low and slowly add the flour just until a shaggy dough comes together. Switch the paddle attachment to a dough attachment and knead the mixture on high speed for 5 to 7 minutes, or until a shiny and elastic dough has formed. Remove the dough, coat the bowl with olive oil, and transfer the dough back into the bowl. Cover with a clean dish towel and set in a warm place for 1 hour, or until doubled in size.

Punch down the dough and divide it into eight equal parts. Roll the pieces into ovals and place on the prepared baking sheet. Wrap in plastic wrap and chill in the refrigerator overnight.

The next morning, remove the rolls from the refrigerator and let sit at room temperature for at least 30 minutes before baking.

Place a metal roasting pan on the bottom rack of the oven and preheat to 450°F [230°C].

Brush the rolls with the remaining 1 Tbsp milk and place in the oven. Add 3 big handfuls of ice cubes to the roasting pan. Bake for 20 to 25 minutes, or until the tops are golden brown. Remove from the oven and serve warm.

Breakfast in Bed

BOARD

Looking for something special to do for your mom this Mother's Day or to surprise a special someone for an anniversary, birthday, or weekend breakfast? Look no further than this breakfast in bed board!

STRATEGY: Personalize it for your favorite person by swapping in their favorite jam or fresh fruit. Add a small vase with flowers to the tray for an extra-special display.

DRINK PAIRING: Serve with both a glass of orange juice and a cup of coffee.

WYATT'S MEATY SUGGESTION: Almost translucent, salty lox has been in the breakfast game for decades. Place thin slices on the bagel with cream cheese, tomatoes, and capers or add ribbons to the frittata.

SERVES 2 (SO YOU CAN EAT WITH THEM)

- 1 cup [120 g] fresh berries
- ½ cup [150 g] berry jam
- 1 Tbsp capers
- 2 Tbsp cream cheese
- Miniature Tomato, Garlic, and Goat Cheese Frittatas (recipe follows)
- 6 tomato slices (from 2 large tomatoes)
- 2 bagels, sliced and toasted

Place the berries in a small bowl. Transfer the capers and cream cheese to a small plate with a serving spoon and a knife. Transfer the frittatas to a small plate along with the tomato slices and bagels. Place everything on a serving tray or platter. Serve right away.

Miniature Tomato, Garlic,
and Goat Cheese Frittatas

Miniature Tomato, Garlic, and Goat Cheese Frittatas

MAKES 6 MINIATURE FRITTATAS

1 tsp olive oil

1 large garlic clove, minced

4 eggs

⅔ cup [160 ml] whole milk

½ tsp fine sea salt

½ tsp freshly ground black pepper

1 tsp chopped fresh thyme
(about 2 sprigs) + more for garnish

1 oz [30 g] fresh goat cheese

4 cherry tomatoes, quartered

Preheat the oven to 375°F [190°C]. Line a twelve-cup muffin tin with six liners.

In a small skillet over medium-low heat, warm the olive oil. Add the garlic and sauté for 30 seconds, or until fragrant. Remove from the heat and set aside.

In a small mixing bowl (or large measuring cup), whisk together the eggs, milk, salt, pepper, and thyme.

Pour the mixture into muffin liners and fill each one three-quarters full. Pinch off small pieces of goat cheese and evenly drop them into the egg mixture. Divide the tomato quarters evenly and drop them into the egg mixture.

Bake for 22 minutes, or until the eggs are set and just beginning to brown on top.

Remove from the oven and let cool for 5 minutes before transferring the frittatas from the muffin tins. Garnish with a few thyme leaves and serve warm.

Part Two:

After

Quick-Pickled Vegetables

Beach

Beach BOARD

This board is all about foods that travel well and are still going to be delicious once you hike out to your favorite beach or lakeshore.

STRATEGY: Since you will most likely have to carry this all to your destination, bring only the amount of servings for the number of people you are planning to feed; the recipe is for six but use the serving guide on page 23 to customize it for your outing. Since there is cheese involved in this board, you'll need to bring a small cooler, which will also be perfect for keeping your beverages in. Don't forget to pack a few knives for cutting the cheese and scooping the spreads, forks for digging out the pickled vegetables, a serving platter or serving board, and a picnic blanket! Transfer the nuts, fig butter, sesame sticks, and crackers in their own resealable containers for easy portability. You can then just arrange them on the board in those containers.

DRINK PAIRING: If you are in a spot that allows alcohol, bring white wine such as Pinot Grigio or Chardonnay. Look for miniature plastic wine bottles. They are ideal for travel and will fit snuggly in a mini cooler.

WYATT'S MEATY SUGGESTION: Bring along a tin of sardines for a portable, affordable, and filling beach snack. Peel the lid back and chow down.

SERVES 6 AS AN APPETIZER

- 6 oz [170 g] hard cheese (such as Manchego or white Cheddar)
- 8 oz [230 g] soft cheese (such as Camembert or mozzarella)
- Quick-Pickled Vegetables (recipe follows)
- 1½ cups [180 g] mixed nuts
- ¼ cup [70 g] fig butter
- 8 oz [230 g] crackers
- 4 oz [115 g] sesame sticks

Lay out a beach blanket and place your board in the very center of the blanket (to try to avoid any sand getting kicked near the food). Place cheese wedges on opposite sides of the board and add serving knives to them. Add open jars of pickled vegetables to the board. Place small serving spoons in the resealable containers of nuts and fig butter and place them on the board. Fill in the remaining space on board with crackers and sesame sticks.

Quick-Pickled Vegetables

Be sure to make these ahead of time—they'll need at least 24 hours in the refrigerator before serving. Quick pickles tend to be less briny, which make them best for eating by themselves or for serving on a cheeseboard. I recommend pairing the carrots and radishes together since they tend to take a little longer to pickle than cucumbers and bell peppers. Give both jars 24 hours to pickle, but you may want to let them sit for longer depending on how you like your pickled veggies.

MAKES 2 PT [910 G]

6 carrots, peeled and cut into 1-in [2.5-cm] chunks

1 bunch small red radishes, tops removed and sliced

4 mini cucumbers, quartered

8 baby bell peppers, halved

8 sprigs fresh dill

2 tsp peppercorns

4 garlic cloves, peeled

2 tsp mustard seeds

2 cups [480 ml] white vinegar

2 cups [480 ml] water

2 Tbsp fine sea salt

¼ cup [50 g] sugar

Place the carrots and radishes in a 1-pt [16-oz] Mason jar, leaving a ½-in [12-mm] gap at the top. Place the cucumbers and bell peppers in another 1-pt [16-oz] Mason jar, leaving a ½-in [12-mm] gap at the top. Divide the dill, peppercorns, garlic, and mustard seeds evenly between the two jars.

In a small saucepan over medium heat, combine the vinegar, water, salt, and sugar. Bring to a boil, stir with a wooden spoon until the sugar and salt dissolve, and remove from the heat. Pour the pickling liquid into the two jars, making sure to completely cover the vegetables. Let cool at room temperature for 1 hour before sealing and transferring to the refrigerator.

Let sit in the refrigerator for at least 24 hours before enjoying.

These pickles should keep for up to 2 weeks if stored in the refrigerator.

Fall BOARD

This board is perfect for a big chilly day gathering or a lazy fall lunch when you need a good carb (focaccia) fix. And the apples and pears topped with blue cheese and honey make for sweet and savory matches that are not to be missed—it's one of my favorite Fall flavor combinations.

STRATEGY: Don't forget to roll your sliced apples and pears in the lemon juice, or they will brown before your guests have a chance to dig in.

DRINK PAIRING: Warm up your favorite cider and put it in six mugs. Garnish with a cinnamon stick when serving.

WYATT'S MEATY SUGGESTION: Bresaola, a lean and musky cured beef, makes a great fall addition because it is often seasoned with nutmeg and cinnamon. If you have trouble finding bresaola, any cured beef or ham would work here.

SERVES 6

3 apples, sliced

3 pears, sliced

1 Tbsp freshly squeezed lemon juice

1-in [2.5-cm] piece honeycomb or ¼ cup [85 g] honey

6 oz [170 g] blue cheese (such as blue Stilton or Gorgonzola)

3 cups [420 g] Smoky Sweet Mixed Nuts (page 201) or store-bought sweet mixed nuts

6 figs, halved

Fall Harvest Focaccia (recipe follows)

Toss the apple slices and pear slices in the lemon juice and add to the serving board. Place the honey in a small serving dish and add it to the board. Fill in all the remaining space with blue cheese, nuts, figs, and focaccia. Add serving knives or spoons for the honey and blue cheese.

Fall
Harvest
Focaccia

Fall Harvest Focaccia

SERVES 6 AS A BOARD COMPONENT

1 heaping tsp active dry yeast

1½ tsp sugar

1 cup [240 ml] warm water (around 110°F / 43°C)

2½ cups [300 g] all-purpose flour

1½ tsp fine sea salt + more for topping

½ cup [120 ml] olive oil + more for drizzling and greasing the bowl

2 Tbsp chopped hazelnuts

1 tsp chopped fresh rosemary

½ cup [80 g] seedless red grapes

Combine the yeast, sugar, and warm water in a small bowl and let sit for 12 minutes, or until bubbly.

In the bowl of a stand mixer fitted with a dough attachment, combine the flour and salt and mix for a few seconds to combine. Add ¼ cup of the olive oil and the yeast mixture and knead on medium speed until the dough comes together, about 30 seconds. Turn the mixer up to medium-high speed and knead for 5 minutes. Remove the dough, coat the mixing bowl in olive oil, and transfer the dough back to the oiled bowl. Cover with a clean dish towel and put in a warm place for 1 hour, or until doubled in size.

Coat a 9-in [23-cm] square baking dish with the remaining ¼ cup olive oil (this is more oil than you normally would use to grease a pan, but it'll yield a crispy crust). Transfer the dough into the prepared baking dish and use clean hands to press the dough into the pan. Turn the dough over to coat the other side with olive oil and continue to press the dough into the pan with your fingertips. Cover and place in a warm spot until doubled in size, about 1 hour.

Preheat the oven to 425°F [220°C].

Once the dough has doubled, press it down one last time with clean fingertips, leaving indents all over the dough. Sprinkle with hazelnuts, rosemary, red grapes, a large pinch of salt, and another drizzle of olive oil. Bake for 20 to 25 minutes, or until golden brown on top.

Remove from the oven and let cool before cutting into squares. Serve warm.

Red, Blue, and Cinnamon PLATTER

Think of this red-and-blue–themed board as the perfect fruit platter for your next Memorial Day, Fourth of July, or Labor Day gathering.

 STRATEGY: Buy the freshest fruit you can find, since you will be serving it raw. You can swap in any red or blue fruit that is in season. Just make sure you are picking fruit with a variety of textures and shapes to keep the board interesting.

 **DRINK PAIRING**: Make white wine spritzers. Keep it simple with two parts wine and one part sparkling water. Garnish with mint or a lime slice.

SERVES 6 AS AN APPETIZER

Sweet Cinnamon Fruit Dip (recipe follows)

1 pt [340 g] strawberries

6 oz [170 g] blueberries

6 oz [170 g] red raspberries

1 cup [140 g] cherries, pitted and halved

Transfer the fruit dip to a small serving bowl and add it to the center of your serving platter. Assemble all fruit pieces on the serving tray or platter around the dip. Serve right away.

Sweet
Cinnamon
Fruit Dip

Sweet Cinnamon Fruit Dip

MAKES 1 HEAPING CUP [295 G]

8 oz [230 g] mascarpone cheese

1 tsp almond extract

1 tsp ground cinnamon

2 Tbsp honey

3 Tbsp whole milk

In a small bowl, whisk together the mascarpone cheese, almond extract, cinnamon, honey, and milk. Serve right away or cover and chill until ready to serve.

Park Picnic SPREAD

Take some time this spring and fall for picnics when the weather is too nice to stay cooped up inside.

STRATEGY : Pack up a blanket, some utensils, a board, and your favorite cheeses and head out on a picnic with friends.

DRINK PAIRING: A light wine like Chardonnay would work great if you are somewhere that allows alcohol. If not, a nice bottle of sparkling water (such as San Pellegrino) is another option.

WYATT'S MEATY SUGGESTION: There are all sorts of meat pâté varieties and any will work well here. Originally created by butchers in the fifteenth century as a way to utilize all parts of the animal, this spread-able meat is now commonly used as picnic fare, as it travels easily and pairs well with cheese.

SERVES 4 AS A HEARTY APPETIZER OR LIGHT MAIN

2 oz [55 g] Cheddar cheese or another semifirm cheese

2 oz [55 g] soft cheese (such as Camembert or mozzarella)

2 oz [55 g] goat cheese

1 lb [455 g] any variety seedless grapes

½ cup [80 g] mixed nuts

20 olives

¼ cup [85 g] honey

Eggplant-Walnut Pâté (recipe follows)

4 oz [115 g] wheat crackers

1 baguette

Lay down a picnic blanket and place your serving board in the middle of the blanket. Place the cheeses and their individual serving knives on the board, leaving enough room around each so that they do not touch. Add the grapes to the board. Place the nuts, olives, honey, and Eggplant-Walnut Pâté in small serving dishes and place them on the board with serving spoons. Serve crackers in a small bowl to the side and place the baguette near the tray (I recommend having guests tear pieces of baguette to enjoy with their servings instead of trying to cut pieces beforehand).

Eggplant-Walnut Pâté

Eggplant-Walnut Pâté

SERVES 4 AS A BOARD COMPONENT

1 large eggplant, halved

1 cup [120 g] toasted walnut halves

1 garlic clove

1 tsp smoked paprika

Fine sea salt

Freshly ground black pepper

1 Tbsp olive oil

Preheat the oven to 375°F [190°C].

Poke the eggplant all over with a fork. Place the eggplant, cut-sides down, on a baking sheet and roast for 30 minutes, or until the inside is very tender. Remove from the oven and let cool a bit.

Once cool enough to handle, scrape the flesh out of the eggplant and place it in a high-speed blender or food processor. Add the walnuts, garlic, smoked paprika, and a dash of salt and pepper. Turn the blender on and slowly add the olive oil while processing. Blend until a creamy dip has formed and no lumps remain. Season with salt and pepper.

Transfer to an airtight container and chill until picnic time. This pâté can be stored in the refrigerator for up to 2 days.

Dog Days of Summer BOARD

This is the perfect raw vegetable plate for when it's too hot to turn on the oven. You'll get a flavor boost from the tahini sauce while enjoying a ton of light and fresh vegetables, so you won't feel bogged down afterward.

STRATEGY: Surround the flavorful dip with a variety of vegetables with different shapes and textures. Make sure to cut the larger vegetables into bite-size pieces, and feel free to swap in your favorite raw vegetables if they aren't already included in the board.

DRINK PAIRING: Light and fruity, a bottle of rosé is the perfect accompaniment for this board.

WYATT'S MEATY SUGGESTION: Pick up Italian dry salami, such as sopressata, for an easy no-cook meat option.

SERVES 8

Tahini Coconut Dipping Sauce (recipe follows)

2 large cucumbers, sliced

8 medium carrots, peeled and sliced

2 bell peppers, cut into strips

4 oz [115 g] snap peas (about 30 pods)

10.5 oz [300 g] cherry tomatoes

1 lb [450 g] broccoli florets

1 lb [450 g] cauliflower florets

Transfer the dipping sauce into a small serving bowl and place on a platter or board. Surround with the vegetables and serve.

Tahini
Coconut
Dipping
Sauce

Tahini Coconut Dipping Sauce

MAKES 2 HEAPING CUPS [580 G]

1 cup [225 g] tahini

¼ cup [72 g] soy or tamari sauce

1 cup unsweetened full-fat coconut milk

½ cup [120 ml] water or vegetable broth + more as needed

2½ Tbsp freshly squeezed lemon juice

1 Tbsp honey

2 heaping tsp chili garlic paste

1 tsp garlic cloves

½ tsp fine sea salt

Freshly ground black pepper

In a high-speed blender, combine the tahini, soy sauce, coconut milk, water, lemon juice, honey, chili garlic paste, garlic, salt, and a dash of pepper and blend until smooth, about 15 seconds. If the sauce is too thick, add more water, 1 Tbsp at a time, until a smooth dipping sauce has formed.

Winter

Carrot Curry Shooters

Solstice

Winter Solstice PLATTER

Treat yourself on a chilly winter afternoon to this platter filled to the brim with winter produce. This board highlights a range of winter's bounty with everything from spiced carrot shooters to juicy oranges to earthy beets.

STRATEGY: Cut the citrus on a separate plate and add it to the board at the end to keep it from dripping liquid onto the rest of the crudités. You can make the Carrot Curry Shooters the night before and then garnish right before serving them warm or chilled.

DRINK PAIRING: Enjoy with a bold, warming red wine like Cabernet Sauvignon.

WYATT'S MEATY SUGGESTION: Add some smoky and rustic flavors to your winter meal by hunting down a local artisan jerky.

SERVES 12 AS AN APPETIZER

Carrot Curry Shooters (recipe follows)

Arils (seeds) from 1 pomegranate

4 blood oranges, peeled and sliced

4 oranges, peeled and sliced

12 figs, halved

6 carrots, peeled and cut into bite-size pieces

2 radishes, sliced thin

2 beets, sliced thin

1 head cauliflower, cut into bite-size florets

Arrange the curry shooters along the center of your platter. Place the pomegranate arils in a small dish and add to the platter. Arrange the fruit and vegetables in the remaining space on the platter.

Carrot Curry Shooters

MAKES 24 SHOOTERS

2 Tbsp unsalted butter

1 lb [450 g] peeled carrots, diced

1 large onion, diced

Fine sea salt

3 garlic cloves

2 tsp curry powder

½ tsp ground turmeric

½ tsp paprika

½ tsp chili powder

1 bay leaf

4 cups [960 ml] vegetable broth

2 cups [480 ml] water

Freshly squeezed lemon juice

Freshly ground black pepper

Plain yogurt, for finishing

Fresh parsley, for garnish

In a large stockpot over medium heat, melt the butter. Add the diced carrots, onion, and a dash of salt. Sauté for about 7 minutes, or until softened. Add the garlic, curry powder, turmeric, paprika, and chili powder, and sauté for another 30 seconds. Add the bay leaf, vegetable broth, water, and another pinch of salt. Bring to a boil, reduce the heat to medium-low, and simmer for 30 minutes.

Remove from the heat and use an immersion blender to blend until smooth, or add to a high-speed blender, in batches if necessary, and blend until smooth. Season with lemon juice, pepper, and more salt.

Divide between twenty-four shooter glasses and drizzle yogurt in a circular motion over the soup. Garnish with parsley and a turn of fresh black pepper. Serve warm or chilled.

Rose & Pistachio
Shortbread

Te

Teatime SPREAD

This sweet spread is a great reminder that sometimes you just need to slow down your afternoon and enjoy some treats and tea with friends.

STRATEGY: If you want to add a savory element to the spread, add a few finger sandwiches, such as cucumber or tuna sandwiches (see Wyatt's meaty suggestion). Include a variety of teas (hibiscus, peppermint, Earl Grey, green tea, chai, etc.) so guests can select their favorite.

DRINK PAIRING: Enjoy the hot tea in a mismatch of vintage teacups, which can be found fairly cheap at local antique shops. A quality vintage teapot is usually a little more pricey but well worth the investment if you indulge in afternoon tea often. If you are extra lucky, you may even have a tea set you inherited from previous generations, and this spread is a perfect excuse to pull that out.

WYATT'S MEATY SUGGESTION: Make tuna sandwiches! Drain a 6-oz [170-g] can of tuna and combine in a small bowl with 1 diced celery stalk, ½ small onion, diced, ¼ cup [60 g] mayonnaise, a squeeze of lemon juice, and salt and pepper. Use four pieces of bread to create two large sandwiches and cut each into four triangle tea sandwiches.

SERVES 6

An array of dried teas

1 lemon, sliced

1 orange, sliced

1 bunch fresh mint

6 tea cakes

6 Cardamom Coffee Cream Scones (page 35) or store-bought scones

6 tea biscuits

Rose and Pistachio Shortbread (recipe follows)

6 Tbsp [90 ml] whole milk

½ cup [110 g] whipped butter

12 sugar cubes

2 cups [600 g] Tomato-Thyme Jam (page 113) or store-bought jam

6 cups [1.4 L] water

Arrange the dried teas on a small platter. Arrange lemon slices, orange slices, and mint on a small platter. Arrange the tea cakes, scones, and tea biscuits on another platter. Place the platters on the serving table. Add milk to a small pitcher and add it to the serving table. Place the whipped butter, sugar cubes, and jam in individual serving bowls with serving spoons or knives and add to the table.

Boil the water and transfer to a teapot. Serve right away with six teacups and six small plates, allowing guests to pick out and make their own teas.

Rose and Pistachio Shortbread

MAKES 32 COOKIES

⅓ cup [45 g] shelled whole pistachios

2 tsp culinary-grade rose petals + more for sprinkling

⅓ cup [65 g] sugar + more for sprinkling

2 cups [280 g] all-purpose flour

1 tsp fine sea salt

1½ tsp rosewater

1 tsp vanilla extract

1 cup [220 g] unsalted butter

In a food processor, pulse the pistachios until finely chopped, 4 or 5 times. Add the rose petals, sugar, flour, and salt and pulse another 2 or 3 times, or until combined. With the food processor running, add the rosewater, vanilla, and butter and process until a large dough ball has formed, about 20 seconds.

Transfer the dough to a clean surface and knead two or three times, or until all the lingering crumbs have been incorporated into the dough. Roll the dough up into a cylinder in wax paper and transfer to the refrigerator to chill for at least 2 hours or up to 24 hours.

Preheat the oven to 350°F [180°C] and line a baking sheet with parchment paper.

Roll the dough out to a thickness of ¼ in [6 mm]. With a biscuit cutter or drinking glass, cut the dough into rounds and transfer them to the prepared baking sheet. Sprinkle with rose petals and sugar. Bake for 12 to 15 minutes, or until browned on the edges.

Remove from the oven and transfer to a wire rack. Let cool completely before serving. Store leftover cookies in an airtight container at room temperature for up to 5 days.

Happ

Ha

Red Wine
Caramelized
Onion Dip

Happy Hour PLATTER

This fuss-free board is the perfect way to start any party!

STRATEGY: Pick a mix of colors and shapes for the vegetables and pile them high on top of each other for a stunning presentation.

DRINK PAIRING: If you don't already have a go-to drink for happy hour, serve a round of simple and classic old-fashioned cocktails. To make, mix 2 oz [60 ml] whiskey with 3 drops Angostura bitters, a splash of club soda, and a sugar cube (or a splash of simple syrup) in an old-fashioned glass. Garnish with a maraschino cherry and an orange peel for an extra pop of color.

WYATT'S MEATY SUGGESTION: Peeled, cooked shrimp is perfect for parties since it doesn't require utensils. Serve with store-bought cocktail sauce or Red Wine Caramelized Onion Dip (but make sure to have two bowls—one for dipping shrimp and one for veggies).

SERVES 12

Red Wine Caramelized Onion Dip (recipe follows)

16 oz [450 g] potato chips

3 cups [400 g] olives

8 oz [230 g] marinated artichoke hearts

16 oz [450 g] crackers

6 cups [960 g] raw vegetables (carrot sticks, celery sticks, radish slices, cherry tomatoes, cauliflower pieces, etc.)

36 store-bought breadsticks

48 oz [1.36 kg] cheese cubes (I used a mixture of pepper Jack and sharp Cheddar cheese for color contrast)

Transfer the dip, potato chips, olives, and marinated artichoke hearts into small dishes and place them on a large serving tray. Fill in the remaining areas on the tray with crackers, vegetables, breadsticks, and cheese cubes. Serve right away with serving spoons and toothpicks.

Red Wine Caramelized Onion Dip

MAKES 4 ½ CUPS [1.17 KG]

¼ cup [60 ml] olive oil

4 large white onions, finely chopped

¼ cup [60 ml] red wine

½ tsp fine sea salt + more as needed

2 cups [480 g] sour cream

1 cup [240 g] Greek yogurt

1 Tbsp tamari or soy sauce

Dash of freshly ground black pepper

In a large saucepan over medium heat, warm the olive oil. Add the onions and sauté for 20 to 25 minutes, stirring often, until golden brown. Add the red wine and sauté until the wine is cooked off, about 10 minutes more. Remove from the heat, add the salt, and let cool.

Once cooled, transfer the onions to a cutting board and finely chop. Transfer to a medium mixing bowl and fold in the sour cream, yogurt, and soy sauce. Season with pepper and more salt, if needed. Cover and transfer to the refrigerator and chill for at least 30 minutes before serving. Can be stored in the refrigerator for up to 3 days.

our

Pink
Hummus

Crostini

Build Your Own Crostini SPREAD

This hands-on board is a fun way to involve your guests. You can make seasonal adjustments by swapping in blackberries, peaches, and basil in the summer; sliced citrus, figs, and tarragon in the fall and winter; and strawberries and chives in the spring. I love to stop at my farmers market the day of the party to see what looks fresh and colorful.

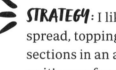

STRATEGY: I like to arrange the base, spread, toppings, and garnish into sections in an assembly line fashion so it's easy for guests to instinctively know how to prepare their crostini. Also, I like to assemble a few and place them in the spread beforehand, as it helps get people's ideas flowing and gives them a few combination suggestions to start with.

If you need to size this board for a group other than twenty, keep in mind that most guests will eat around six crostini throughout the night, and for each crostini you'll want to have 1½ Tbsp of spread, 2 or 3 toppings, and 1 tsp of garnish.

DRINK PAIRING: Serve with a red wine spritzer. It's fancy enough for a cocktail party but light enough for a small get-together. To make, mix two parts dry red wine (such as a Merlot or Shiraz) with one part sparkling water and serve with a slice of orange.

WYATT'S MEATY SUGGESTION: In keeping with the Italian origins of crostini, turn to capocollo or coppa. These Italian cured meats boast a little more brawn than prosciutto and a little more elegance than salami.

Base pieces:

2 batches Quick Crostini (page 198)

Spreads:

Pink Hummus (recipe follows)

1 cup [290 g] store-bought fig butter or jam

1 cup [260 g] peanut or almond butter

8 oz [230 g] cream cheese or chèvre

1 cup [220 g] Compound Butters Three Ways (pages 217–218)

1 cup [240 g] Whole-Grain Ale Mustard (page 209) or store-bought whole-grain mustard

1 cup [250 g] Pistachio Herb Pesto (page 210) or store-bought pesto

10 oz [285 g] store-bought olive tapenade

1 cup [240 g] mascarpone cheese

8 oz [230 g] soft cheese (such as Camembert or mozzarella), sliced

Toppings:

3 cups [420 g] sliced fruit (peaches, figs, berries, etc.)

Three 8-oz [230-g] variety packs of sliced cheese (about 12 slices each, large enough to halve or quarter)

2 cups [150 g] sliced radishes

2 cups [140 g] carrot batons (large matchstick pieces)

1½ cups [165 g] chopped nuts (pecans, almonds, walnuts)

2 cups [300 g] cucumber slices

6 oz [170 g] sun-dried tomatoes

One 16-oz [455-g] jar of roasted red peppers, drained and chopped

Garnishes:

1 cup [40 g] chopped fresh herbs (such as basil, mint, parsley, or cilantro)

1 cup [120 g] crushed pistachios

¼ cup [60 ml] balsamic glaze

¼ cup [60 ml] olive oil

¼ cup [85 g] honey

2 Tbsp red pepper flakes

2 Tbsp ground cinnamon

2 Tbsp flaky flavored salt (such as garlic salt, lemon salt, or red wine salt)

Place all the ingredients into individual bowls and/or small plates. Place the plates and utensils on the side of the table you want guests to start on. Next to those, place the base pieces followed by spreads, toppings, and garnishes. Add a serving spoon or fork into each bowl and serve.

Pink Hummus

MAKES 1¼ CUPS [300 G]

One 15-oz [425 g] can chickpeas, drained

¼ cup [60 ml] pickled beet juice

2 Tbsp olive oil + more for garnish

¼ cup [55 g] tahini

1 garlic clove

½ tsp fine sea salt + more as needed

Freshly ground black pepper

Chopped fresh parsley, for garnish

In a food processor, place the chickpeas, beet juice, olive oil, tahini, garlic, and salt and process until completely smooth, 2 to 3 minutes. Season with pepper and more salt. Transfer to a shallow serving bowl, drizzle with olive oil, and sprinkle with parsley. Store in an airtight container in the refrigerator for up to 3 days.

Part Three:

Eveni

Holiday
Hos

Mini Cheeseballs

Holiday Hosting

SPREAD

These bite-size appetizers add variety and texture to a big platter presentation and allow your guests to try several different flavors. And each of your guests can take an entire mini cheeseball for their plate instead of fiddling with a large appetizer at the serving area.

STRATEGY: Make the cheeseballs the morning of your event (or the night before) and just roll them in their toppings right before guests arrive.

DRINK PAIRING: Serve with a festively dark and rich wine like Syrah or Shiraz.

WYATT'S MEATY SUGGESTION: Is bacon ever not the answer? Swap ½ cup [40 g] crumbled bacon with the chopped pistachio in the Mini Cheeseball recipe that follows to create a bacon and herb coating.

SERVES 10 TO 12

Mini Cheeseballs (recipe follows)

20 carrot batons (large matchstick pieces from about 5 large carrots)

20 celery sticks (from about 6 celery stalks)

20 radish slices (from about 4 small radishes)

8 oz [230 g] sesame sticks

8 oz [230 g] crackers

3 cups [420 g] mixed nuts

Quick Crostini (page 198)

Pile cheeseballs on the platter so that they are grouped based on what they are rolled in. Fill the empty space with carrot slices, celery sticks, radish slices, sesame sticks, crackers, and crostini.

Mini Cheeseballs

MAKES 40 CHEESEBALLS

Two 8-oz [230-g] packages cream cheese, at room temperature

2 Tbsp crème fraîche

2 tsp Worcestershire sauce (vegetarian, if you can find it)

⅔ cup [50 g] shredded white Cheddar cheese

⅔ cup [55 g] shredded hard cheese (such as Gruyère or Parmesan)

Fine sea salt

Freshly ground black pepper

¼ cup + 1 Tbsp [30 g] crumbled blue cheese

½ cup + 2 Tbsp [65 g] chopped pecans

¼ cup [35 g] chopped dried apricots

½ cup [60 g] slivered almonds

½ cup [50 g] chopped pistachios

¼ cup [32 g] chopped fresh herbs (such as thyme, sage, rosemary, etc.)

Line a baking sheet with parchment paper.

Use a sturdy spatula to mix together the cream cheese, crème fraîche, Worcestershire sauce, Cheddar cheese, and Gruyère. Season with salt and pepper.

Use a 1-in [2.5-cm] cookie scoop to portion out a ball of the cheese mixture. Roll the ball between your wet hands to create an evenly spherical cheeseball and place it on the prepared baking sheet. Repeat with the rest of the cheese mixture. Cover and let chill for at least 2 hours.

Set out three shallow dishes. Mix together the blue cheese and chopped pecans in one dish, apricots and almond pieces in another, and pistachios and herbs in the last. Remove the cheeseballs from the refrigerator and roll each ball in one of the mixtures until completely coated. Transfer to a serving platter and repeat with the rest of the cheeseballs. Let sit at room temperature for at least 20 minutes before serving.

Date Night SPREAD

This romantic board for two is sure to set the mood for date night.

 STRATEGY: Make sure you avoid stinky cheeses or garlic-spiked elements for this board, as smelly breath is never good on date night. The chocolate-covered strawberries will make more than two servings, but you might as well make the whole batch, since you usually have to buy strawberries by the pound anyway; save the rest for later or give the extras to friends to enjoy. Have two separate boards that you place the food on: one for sweets and one for savory.

 **DRINK PAIRING**: Keep it classy and simple with a dark red wine like Merlot.

 WYATT'S MEATY SUGGESTION: Transform your date night into an Italian delight by adding the famously luscious cured ham, prosciutto. For a pretty presentation, twirl the slices into a rose.

SERVES 2 AS A LIGHT MEAL OR HEARTY APPETIZER

Dark Chocolate–Covered Strawberries with Pistachio and Raspberry Dust (recipe follows)

4 chocolate truffles

1-in [2.5-cm] piece honeycomb or ¼ cup [85 g] honey

2 oz [55 g] smoked Gouda

2-oz [55-g] log goat cheese

4 oz [115 g] wheat crackers

2 oz [55 g] sesame sticks

Place two fairly large boards on your serving table and cluster the Dark Chocolate–Covered Strawberries with Pistachio and Raspberry Dust, and chocolate truffles on one of them. Place the honeycomb in a small dish and add to the same board. On the remaining board, add the Gouda, goat cheese, and wheat crackers. Place the sesame sticks in a small bowl and add to the savory board. Serve right away.

Dark Chocolate–Covered Strawberries with Pistachio and Raspberry Dust

Dark Chocolate–Covered Strawberries with Pistachio and Raspberry Dust

MAKES 18 TO 20 STRAWBERRIES

⅓ **cup [12 g] dried raspberries**

⅓ **cup [40 g] shelled pistachios**

8 oz [230 g] dark chocolate chunks

16 oz [455 g] strawberries, washed and patted dry

In a high-speed blender, blend the dried raspberries until finely ground, about 3 seconds. Transfer to a small shallow dish. Rinse and dry out the blender and add the pistachios. Blend until finely ground, about 5 seconds. Transfer to a shallow dish.

Line a baking sheet with wax paper and set aside.

Add about 2 in [5 cm] of water to a medium saucepan and bring to a boil. Once boiling, remove from the heat and place a double boiler (or heat-proof bowl) over the water and add three-quarters of the chocolate. Use a spatula to stir the chocolate until most of it has melted. Keep a candy thermometer in the chocolate and remove the bowl from the water if it gets warmer than 90°F [30°C]. Keep stirring until almost all the chocolate has melted. Add the remaining one-quarter of the chocolate and continue to stir until completely melted and glossy.

Holding a strawberry by the stem, dip it into the chocolate, roll it into the ground pistachios, roll in the raspberry dust, and transfer it to the prepared baking sheet. Repeat with the rest of the strawberries.

Set aside and let harden completely before serving, about 1 hour.

Movie Night BOARD

Spoil yourself with this board the next time you decide to stay in for a movie marathon with friends.

STRATEGY: Have these simple snacks ready to go for when you press play. Having trouble finding reputable Cheddar cheese powder at your local grocery store? No problem: Use the cheese packet that comes in boxed macaroni and cheese (and then save the pasta for another use).

DRINK PAIRING: Drink your dessert by serving root beer floats during intermission.

WYATT'S MEATY SUGGESTION: Pepperoni is more than just a pizza topping. Try it with crackers for easy movie grub.

SERVES 6

Chicago-Style Caramel and Cheddar Popcorn (recipe follows)

3 cups [360 to 480 g] fruit (sliced apples, blueberries, pineapple chunks, banana pieces, etc.)

1 cup [180 g] chocolate pieces (such as peanut butter cups, malt balls, nonpareils, chocolate-covered pretzels, etc.)

1½ cups [210 g] Smoky Sweet Mixed Nuts (page 201) or store-bought mixed nuts

6 oz [170 g] cheese cubes (such as Colby Jack or Cheddar cheese)

1½ cups [85 g] Chex Mix (store-bought or use your favorite recipe)

Place the popcorn, fruit slices, chocolate pieces, mixed nuts, cheese cubes, and Chex Mix in individual bowls and transfer to a tray. Serve right away.

Chicago-Style
Caramel &
Cheddar Popcorn

Chicago-Style Caramel and Cheddar Popcorn

SERVES 6 AS A BOARD COMPONENT

2 Tbsp peanut oil

½ cup [100 g] popcorn kernels

Caramel Popcorn:

**½ cup [90 g] lightly packed brown
 sugar**

¼ cup [80 g] corn syrup

4 Tbsp [55 g] unsalted butter

½ tsp fine sea salt

½ tsp baking soda

½ tsp vanilla extract

Cheddar Popcorn:

2 Tbsp unsalted butter

¼ cup [30 g] Cheddar cheese powder

½ tsp mustard powder

Dash of smoked paprika

Dash of fine sea salt

Pour the oil into a large stockpot or saucepan fitted with a lid and place over medium heat. Add two popcorn kernels and let sit until they pop. Once popped, add the remaining kernels, cover, and gently shake the pot back and forth over the heat to toss the kernels as they pop. Continue doing this until all the kernels are popped, which is easiest to determine when there is a 2- or 3-second pause between pops. The time will vary based on how hot your stove is and what kind of pot you are using. Remove from the heat and divide the popcorn evenly between two bowls.

Preheat the oven to 250°F [120°C] and butter a rimmed baking pan.

To make the caramel corn, add half the popcorn to the prepared baking pan.

Add the brown sugar, corn syrup, butter, and salt to a medium saucepan. Whisk the ingredients together over medium heat until the mixture begins to bubble. Let boil, uninterrupted (no stirring), for 5 minutes, or until the mixture turns a deep brown.

Remove from the heat and immediately whisk in the baking soda and vanilla. Working quickly, pour the caramel over the popcorn in the prepared rimmed baking pan and use two large spoons to mix the popcorn around in the caramel until it's completely coated. Transfer to the oven and bake for 30 minutes, tossing halfway through.

Remove from the oven and let cool before serving.

Meanwhile, to make the Cheddar popcorn, melt the butter in a small saucepan over medium heat. Pour over the remaining popcorn in the bowl and toss to coat. Add the Cheddar powder, mustard powder, paprika, and salt and toss until completely coated.

To serve, combine the caramel and Cheddar popcorns in a large bowl and toss to mix. Best enjoyed right away.

Grill

Charred Romaine Wedges with
Tarragon-Buttermilk Dressing

Out

Grill Out PLATTER

Take advantage of the next beautiful summer evening by inviting a few friends over and firing up your grill! This huge grilled veggie platter is all you need for your next cookout (well, that and a cold six-pack).

STRATEGY: If it's early in the season, feel free to swap in asparagus for corn and any other veggies you prefer to grill. We have a charcoal grill that we use to make this platter. To measure the temperature of our charcoal grill, we use the "hand test." Hold your hand about 4 in [10 cm] above the coals and see how long you can comfortably keep it there. For medium heat, it should be 5 or 6 seconds, and for low heat, 8 to 10 seconds. And don't forget to check the food often to avoid burning.

DRINK PAIRING: Keep things light and refreshing with an ice-cold blonde ale.

WYATT'S MEATY SUGGESTION: As an all-American classic cookout food, brats are a flavorful yet easy option for the grill.

SERVES 6

1 cup [240 ml] olive oil

½ cup [120 ml] white wine vinegar

1½ Tbsp dried oregano

1 tsp red pepper flakes

1 tsp fine sea salt

Freshly ground black pepper

1 bunch whole peeled carrots

3 ears husked corn, halved crosswise

1½ lb [680 g] red potatoes

2 bell peppers, quartered

12 oz [340 g] cherry tomatoes

1 medium onion, quartered

1 large zucchini, cut into 1-in [2.5-cm] pieces

Charred Romaine Wedges with Tarragon-Buttermilk Dressing (recipe follows)

Whisk together the olive oil, vinegar, oregano, red pepper flakes, salt, and pepper. Divide between two resealable freezer bags and add the carrots, corn, potatoes, peppers, tomatoes, onions, and zucchini. Let marinate in the refrigerator for at least 1 hour or up to 4 hours.

Preheat a charcoal grill to low heat, using the hand test as a guide to let you know when it's ready.

Transfer the vegetables from the marinade to a grilling basket and place on the grill. Cook, tossing often, until the vegetables begin to brown (time will vary greatly depending on how hot your grill is, so watch them carefully). Transfer the grilled vegetables to a serving tray and serve right away.

Charred Romaine Wedges with Tarragon-Buttermilk Dressing

SERVES 6 AS A BOARD COMPONENT

½ cup [120 ml] buttermilk

¼ cup [60 g] sour cream

2 tsp fresh tarragon

Juice and zest from ½ lemon

1 garlic clove, minced

Dash of fine sea salt

Dash of freshly ground black pepper

1 Tbsp olive oil

2 large heads romaine lettuce

In a small bowl, whisk together the buttermilk, sour cream, tarragon, lemon zest, lemon juice, garlic, salt, and pepper and let chill in the refrigerator for at least 30 minutes before serving.

Preheat a charcoal grill to low heat, using the hand test as a guide to let you know when it's ready.

Brush the olive oil on the romaine. Place the romaine heads on the grill and let roast for 1 to 2 minutes on each side, or just until charred around the outside.

For a stunning presentation, transfer to a plate and let guests pull off layers of romaine and drizzle with dressing. Alternatively, chop the romaine into large chunks and drizzle with dressing before serving.

Lazy

Tomato-
Thyme Jam

Dinner

Lazy Dinner

SMORGASBORD

Delicious dinners don't have to take hours to prepare! The key to this dinner is using fresh produce and high-quality ingredients, as fare that can shine on its own doesn't need a lot of prep and fuss.

STRATEGY : Prepare the jam and chop the veggies ahead of time for an even quicker assembly come dinnertime.

DRINK PAIRING: I suggest enjoying this board with a light cocktail like a gin and tonic. The two-ingredient drink is simple to whip up and won't overpower the flavors on your board.

WYATT'S MEATY SUGGESTION: Serve salami on this board. The cured sausage is an essential go-to for those of us who don't feel like cooking meat, and it can top anything (although I recommend baguette slices). It requires no preparation for your lazy evening—slice it up, munch it down.

SERVES 2 AS A MAIN

½ cup [225 g] hummus

½ cup [70 g] raw almonds

½ cup [150 g] Tomato-Thyme Jam (recipe follows) or savory store-bought jelly (such as jalapeño jelly)

8 oz [230 g] olives or 4 oz [115 g] sweet pickles

3 oz [85 g] goat cheese

12 toasted baguette slices, or 6 slices of toasted bread

½ pt [6 oz / 170 g] cherry tomatoes, sliced

4 medium peeled carrots, chopped

1 bell pepper, sliced

Fine sea salt in a shaker

Fresh black peppercorns in a mill

Transfer the goat cheese, hummus, almonds, jam, and olives or sweet pickles to their own individual bowls and place on the table. Transfer baguette slices, tomatoes, carrots, and bell peppers onto individual plates and add to table. Add the salt shaker and pepper mill to the table. Serve right away by having your guests dip the vegetables in hummus or savory jam and topping the bread with vegetables, jams, olives, and goat cheese.

Tomato-Thyme Jam

MAKES ABOUT 1 CUP [300 G]

½ **cup [100 g] sugar**

½ **Tbsp fresh thyme leaves**

**About 10 Roma tomatoes,
cored and quartered**

**3 Tbsp freshly squeezed lemon juice
(from about 1 lemon)**

**1 tsp fresh lemon zest (from about
1 lemon)**

1 tsp fine sea salt

½ **tsp freshly ground black pepper**

In a food processor, pulse the sugar and thyme leaves for 15 seconds, until fragrant and the thyme is evenly mixed throughout the sugar. Add the tomatoes, lemon juice and zest, salt, and pepper and pulse for an additional 15 seconds, or until the sugar has dissolved.

Transfer the tomato mixture to a 12-in [30.5-cm] nonstick skillet. Bring to a boil over high heat and let boil, stirring occasionally, until reduced by half, about 10 minutes. Turn the heat to medium-high and cook for an additional 10 to 12 minutes, stirring often, until it reaches the consistency of jam and becomes glossy.

Remove from the heat and let cool. Season with salt and pepper. Serve right away or store in an airtight container in the refrigerator for up to 7 days.

Dinner Party SPREAD

Bring your party cheese spread to a whole new level with a cheese "cake." A common sight at weddings, this cheese tier adds height and an extra-fun presentation to your table.

 STRATEGY: I did the servings a little differently for this board because no two dinner parties are the same, and I'd love for you to use this board for a party of any size. The serving instructions here are for one person, so just multiply the ingredients by the number of guests and voilà—you are ready to (start prepping for your) party! The Tiered Cheese "Cake" is going to be the star of the show for this presentation, so keep your additional items simple with edibles that will complement the cheeses.

 **DRINK PAIRING**: Call in an elegant white wine for this spread, such as Sauvignon Blanc.

 WYATT'S MEATY SUGGESTION: Serve slices of crowd-pleasing summer sausage. It's an American favorite and pairs wonderfully with cheese and crackers.

SERVES 1 AS AN APPETIZER (MULTI-PLY BY THE NUMBER OF GUESTS)

Tiered Cheese "Cake" (preparation and portioning follows)

1 oz [30 g] crackers

3 or 4 pieces of Quick Crostini (page 198) or store-bought crostini

2 Tbsp [20 g] mixed nuts

1 Tbsp [20 g] honey

Place the Tiered Cheese "Cake" in the center of the serving table. Put the crackers, crostini, mixed nuts, and honey in individual bowls and assemble around the tiered cheeses.

Tiered
Cheese
"Cake"

Tiered Cheese "Cake"

A few pointers to keep in mind when building a Tiered Cheese "Cake":

- Plan to have about 1½ oz [40 g] of cheese per guest—this should be the total for all the cheeses, not just per variety.

- I'd recommend between 3 and 5 cheese wheels, depending on the size of your party and how big of a presentation you want to create.

- Consider taste, texture, and price point when picking out your cheeses. Try to combine hard, soft, and blue-veined cheeses so that there is a variety sure to please any guest. If possible, visit a cheese shop so you can sample the cheeses and ask as many questions as you need to.

- Choose cheese wheels that look good with each other and make sure each layer is at least 1 in [2.5 cm] wider than the layer above it.

How to Assemble

Select a serving surface (a large shallow bowl, platter, cheese plate, etc.) and stack the cheese wheels on top of each other, starting with the widest as the base and moving up. From there, add any garnishes you'd like around the tiers, such as edible flowers, nontoxic foliage, fresh herbs, figs, or seedless grapes, and make sure to set cheese knives for each layer nearby.

Hot Chocolate TRAY

Warm your guests with a spread of hot chocolate and all the toppings you could think of to deck it out.

 STRATEGY: Serve this board with White Chocolate Hot Cocoa (recipe follows) or add hot chocolate packets to your tray if you'd rather have the guests put it together themselves. If you're making this tray for children, omit the amaretto from the whipped cream and throw in a splash of almond extract instead. Provide wood or plastic stirrers for stirring in the mix-ins.

SERVES 4

2 Tbsp milk chocolate shavings

2 Tbsp dark chocolate shavings

2 Tbsp white chocolate shavings

2 Tbsp colorful sprinkles

½ cup [60 g] chopped nuts (such as pecans, pistachios, or peanuts)

1 tsp Dutch-process cocoa powder, for dusting

¼ cup [120 g] toffee pieces

2 oz [55 g] semisweet chocolate chips

8 cookies (such as Pirouline rolled wafers or stroopwafel caramel waffle cookies)

White Chocolate Hot Cocoa with Amaretto Whipped Cream (recipe follows)

Place the different chocolate shavings, sprinkles, nuts, cocoa powder, toffee pieces, and chocolate chips in individual bowls and assemble on a tray. Add a small spoon to each bowl. Place the cookies on the tray and serve with the hot cocoa, encouraging your guests to dip the cookies in their drinks or enjoy them between sips.

White Chocolate Hot Cocoa with Amaretto Whipped Cream

White Chocolate Hot Cocoa with Amaretto Whipped Cream

SERVES 4

Hot Cocoa:
3 cups [720 ml] whole milk

1 cup [240 ml] heavy cream

6 oz [170 g] white chocolate, cut into pieces

½ tsp vanilla extract

Pinch of fine sea salt

4 shots of amaretto liqueur (optional)

Whipped Cream:
¾ cup [180 ml] heavy cream

1 Tbsp sugar

1 Tbsp amaretto liqueur

Place a mixing bowl and whisk attachment in the freezer for 15 minutes before starting.

To make the hot cocoa, combine the whole milk and heavy cream in a medium saucepan over medium heat. Let heat, stirring occasionally, just until the edges of the milk mixture start to bubble. Once bubbling, remove from the heat and toss in the white chocolate, vanilla, and salt. Stir until the white chocolate has completely melted.

To make the whipped cream, affix the chilled mixing bowl and whisk attachment to the stand mixer and combine the heavy cream, sugar, and amaretto in the bowl. Whisk at medium speed until firm peaks form, about 7 to 10 minutes.

To serve, divide the hot cocoa among four mugs and add a shot of amaretto, if desired for a boozy adult treat, into each serving. Dollop whip cream over the cocoas and serve right away.

Holiday Sweet Treat

Soft Chocolate
Ginger Cookies

Holiday Sweet Treat SPREAD

This spread is like the cookie plate you leave out for Santa but taken to a whole new level. In this collaborative spread, your guests participate in the baking, so you end up with a variety of treats that will change every time you throw a new party.

STRATEGY: Ask all your guests to bring a dozen homemade cookies or treats so that you can make a big spread of homemade sweets without having to spend days baking. My recipe for ginger cookies yields three dozen because I prefer to have too much—especially when it's something like sweets that will stay good for days. Reserve a small table for the spread and have three large platters to sort the treats: a platter for candies (candy canes, truffles, mints, etc.), chocolate cookies (in case they melt into each other), and a platter for all other cookies and cakes.

DRINK PAIRING: Serve a pot each of decaf coffee, regular coffee, and a batch of peppermint tea. This will make sure you are pleasing everyone no matter what their drink of choice is, and they all go wonderfully with sweets.

SERVES 1 (MULTIPLY BY THE NUMBER OF GUESTS)

- **3 pieces of candy (such as peppermint sticks, gummy bears, Swedish fish, gumdrops, rock candy, etc.)**
- **3 chocolate cookies (such as Soft Chocolate Ginger Cookies, recipe follows)**
- **3 non-chocolate cookies (such as shortbread, linzer cookies, or sugar cookies)**

Place three trays onto your serving table. Add candy to one tray, chocolate cookies to the second, and non-chocolate cookies to the third tray. Make sure to explain to guests the system for when they add their contributions to the spread.

Soft Chocolate Ginger Cookies

- ¾ cup [165 g] unsalted butter, at room temperature
- 1 cup [180 g] lightly packed brown sugar
- 1 egg
- 1 tsp vanilla extract
- ¼ cup [80 g] molasses
- 2 cups [240 g] all-purpose flour
- ¼ cup [25 g] natural cocoa powder
- 2 tsp ground ginger
- 1 tsp baking soda
- 1 tsp ground cinnamon
- ½ tsp ground nutmeg
- ¼ tsp fine sea salt
- ¼ cup [50 g] sugar

Preheat the oven to 350°F [180°C] and line two large baking sheets with parchment paper.

Add the butter and brown sugar to a large mixing bowl and beat with a hand mixer on medium speed until fluffy and light, about 2 minutes. With the mixer running, add the egg and mix until combined. Add the vanilla and molasses and mix until combined.

In a small mixing bowl, whisk together the flour, cocoa powder, ginger, baking soda, cinnamon, nutmeg, and salt.

With the mixer on low speed, slowly mix the flour mixture into the butter mixture. Once the flour is mostly mixed in, turn the speed to medium and mix for 1 minute more, or until completely combined.

Put the sugar in a small, shallow dish. Use a 1-in [2.5-cm] cookie scoop to grab a heaping scoop of dough and roll it into a 1½-in [4-cm] ball between your hands. Roll the dough ball in the sugar and place it on the prepared baking sheet. Repeat with the rest of the dough, spacing the dough balls 2 in [5 cm] apart on the prepared baking sheets.

Bake for 12 minutes, rotating halfway through, until they begin to darken. Transfer to a cooling rack and let cool completely before serving. The cookies will crisp up on the outside as they cool and remain gooey soft on the inside. Store in an airtight container for up to 2 days.

mores

Spiced Chai
Graham Crackers

S'mores SMORGASBORD

Light up the backyard fire pit and roast up a batch of s'mores with neighbors and friends on a starlit evening. Or, for you city dwellers, start up that patio grill (or even gas stove!) and pretend like you are on a wilderness camping trip with this smorgasbord.

STRATEGY: Everyone is always impressed when I bring my own homemade graham crackers to a gathering. They are great for bonfires because you can make them a few days ahead of time and save yourself some prep on the day of your gathering. If you want to keep this board vegetarian, seek out gelatin-free marshmallows.

DRINK PAIRING: Cut through each sweet bite with a big mug of hot peppermint tea. It'll also keep you warm on cool fall evenings and aid in boosting your immune system.

WYATT'S MEATY SUGGESTION: Grab a stick and roast some hot dogs. Roasting weenies over a fire will yield a crispy-on-the-outside, juicy-on-the-inside dog. Plus, they are inexpensive and always a crowd pleaser.

SERVES 12

12 marshmallows

Spiced Chai Graham Crackers (recipe follows) or store-bought graham crackers

Twelve 3-in [7.5-cm] square pieces of chocolate (consider an assortment like dark chocolate, milk chocolate, white chocolate, white chocolate with peppermint, etc.)

3 cups [270 to 330 g] toppings (such as chopped nuts, sliced strawberries, butterscotch chips, toasted coconut, jam, fresh mint, etc.)

Lay the marshmallows down in the center of the platter or tray. Group the crackers, chocolate, and toppings together around the marshmallows, filling in the outer portions of the tray.

Invite guests to roast individual marshmallows over an open flame. To make open-face sandwiches: Lay one piece of chocolate over one graham cracker, add the hot marshmallow, and sprinkle with the toppings of their choice.

Spiced Chai Graham Crackers

MAKES 12 CRACKERS

6 Tbsp [90 ml] whole milk

⅓ cup [115 g] honey

1 black tea bag

1 Tbsp vanilla extract

2½ cups [280 g] all-purpose flour + more for the work surface

1 cup [200 g] lightly packed brown sugar

2 tsp ground cinnamon

1 tsp baking soda

1 tsp ground ginger

1 tsp ground cardamom

½ tsp ground allspice

½ tsp fine sea salt

¼ tsp freshly ground black pepper

8 Tbsp [110 g] cold unsalted butter, cut into small cubes

Coarse sugar (optional)

In a small saucepan, heat the milk and honey over medium-low heat until it just starts to simmer, whisking often to make sure the honey is dissolved. Turn the heat off, add the tea bag and vanilla, cover, and let steep for 5 minutes. Remove and discard the tea bag and set the milk mixture aside.

In a food processor, combine the flour, brown sugar, cinnamon, baking soda, ginger, cardamom, allspice, salt, and pepper, and pulse until combined.

Add the butter and pulse until a coarse meal forms.

With the processor running, slowly pour in the milk mixture and process until a big sticky dough ball forms, 3 to 5 minutes.

Place the dough between two long sheets of wax paper and, using a rolling pin, roll the dough into a 12-in [30.5-cm] square. Transfer the wax paper and dough to a baking sheet and freeze until firm, about 20 minutes.

Line two baking sheets with parchment paper.

Remove the chilled dough from the freezer and divide into two pieces. Transfer the dough to a floured surface and roll each piece into a 12-by-16-in [30.5-by-40.5-cm] rectangle that's about ⅛ in [4 mm] thick. Cut the rectangles into 4-in [10-cm] squares and transfer to the prepared baking sheets. Freeze the dough until firm, at least 30 minutes or up to overnight.

Preheat the oven to 350°F [180°C].

Bake the cookies until firm, 20 to 25 minutes. Remove from the oven, sprinkle with coarse sugar (if using), and let cool completely. Store in an airtight container for up to 3 days.

Hallow

Mulled Cider

een

Halloween BOARD

Handing out candy on Halloween can be exhausting and isn't nearly as fun to do solo. To make it more exciting, invite a few friends over to help dole out treats and thank them by serving this board. The scent from the mulled cider alone will be enough to get you in the Halloween spirit.

STRATEGY: Make sure to toss the apple slices and pears in lemon juice so they don't brown.

For vegetarians: If you can't find vegetarian cheese curd, cubed vegetarian Swiss or Cheddar cheese work great here as well.

DRINK PAIRING: Make the Mulled Cider (recipe follows) in a slow cooker if you have the time beforehand and want a more hands-off approach, or make it on the stove for a quick fix (both options will have your kitchen smelling like fall).

WYATT'S MEATY SUGGESTION: For an easy meat pairing, buy frozen meatballs and heat them according to the package directions. Fancy them up by adding your favorite barbecue or tomato-based sauce and serve with toothpicks for spearing.

SERVES 8 AS AN APPETIZER

- 4 oz [115 g] blue cheese (such as Gorgonzola or blue Stilton)
- 8 oz [230 g] cheese curds
- 4 oz [115 g] smoked Gouda
- 1-in [2.5-cm] piece honeycomb or ¼ cup [85 g] honey
- 4 apples, sliced
- 4 pears, sliced
- 1 Tbsp freshly squeezed lemon juice
- 2 cups [240 g] walnut halves
- 8 fresh Mission figs
- 2 cups [320 g] seedless grapes
- Mulled Cider (recipe follows)

Place the cheeses evenly across the board so that none are touching. Add the honey to a small dish and place on the board. Toss the apple and pear slices with lemon juice in a small bowl and then place the slices on empty spaces on the board. Fill in the remaining empty spots with walnuts, figs, and grapes.

Enjoy by topping the pear and apple slices with blue cheese, cheese curds, or Gouda and a drizzle of honey while enjoying nibbles of figs, walnuts, and grapes in between.

Mulled Cider

SERVES 8

8 cups [1.9 L] apple cider

10 allspice berries

8 whole cloves

½ vanilla bean

3 cinnamon sticks

4 cardamom pods

1 orange, sliced + 8 slices for serving

½ cup [120 ml] rum (optional)

Quick stove-top version: Add the cider, allspice, cloves, vanilla bean, cinnamon sticks, cardamom, and orange slices to a large stockpot. Bring to a simmer over medium-high heat. Cover, turn the heat to low, and let simmer for 20 minutes. Use a fine-mesh strainer to strain the spices and orange slices from the cider, and add rum (if using). Pour into eight serving mugs, garnish each with an orange slice, and serve warm.

Extra-flavorful slow-cooker version: Put the cider, allspice, cloves, vanilla bean, cinnamon sticks, cardamom, and orange slices in a slow cooker and cook on high heat, covered, for 1½ to 2 hours, or on low heat, covered, for 3 to 4 hours. Use a fine-mesh strainer to strain the spices and orange from the cider, and add rum (if using). Pour into eight serving mugs, garnish each with an orange slice, and serve warm.

Whipped Feta with
Black Sesame Seeds

Black-Tie

Black-Tie SPREAD

This black-tie board is the perfect classy starter for your next fancy dinner party or for New Year's Eve. All the food is black and white for a unique presentation.

STRATEGY: To stick to the black-and-white theme, select light-colored crackers. If you can't find black sesame seeds for the whipped feta, poppy seeds will also work. Also, if possible, pick out black and white plates and silverware.

DRINK PAIRING: Serve with a bottle of bubbly champagne; it's the perfect drink to celebrate ringing in the New Year (or any other momentous occasion)!

WYATT'S MEATY SUGGESTION: It may break the bank, but try to pick up a little bit of caviar (fish roe). It's a salty, briny delicacy meant for special occasions, and there are some delicious regional options you don't have to be a czar to enjoy, such as salmon, paddlefish, or American white sturgeon.

SERVES 12 AS AN APPETIZER

Whipped Feta with Black Sesame Seeds (recipe follows)

6 oz [170 g] soft white cheese (such as Camembert or mozzarella)

4 white radishes, sliced

1 head cauliflower, chopped into bite-size florets

8 oz [230 g] light-colored crackers

1 pumpernickel loaf, cut into bite-size pieces and toasted

36 black olives

12 dark chocolate truffles

12 white chocolate truffles

Place the whipped feta in a serving bowl. Place it on one side of the board and the soft cheese on the opposite side of the board. Surround the cheeses with radishes, cauliflower, crackers, pumpernickel bread, and olives. Place the truffles on a separate board or serving plate near the savory board. Serve right away.

Whipped Feta with Black Sesame Seeds

SERVES 12 AS A BOARD COMPONENT

12 oz [340 g] feta

4 oz [115 g] cream cheese

6 Tbsp [90 ml] heavy cream

1½ tsp black sesame seeds

In a food processor, pulse the feta until finely crumbled, about 3 seconds. Add the cream cheese and pulse until the cheese mixture is combined and starts to become smooth, about 10 seconds. With the food processor running, slowly pour in the heavy cream until a light and fluffy dip has formed, about 15 seconds.

Transfer the dip to a serving bowl, cover, and chill in the refrigerator until ready to serve. When ready to serve, uncover and sprinkle with black sesame seeds.

The dip should keep for up to 2 days in an airtight container in the refrigerator, but best enjoyed same day.

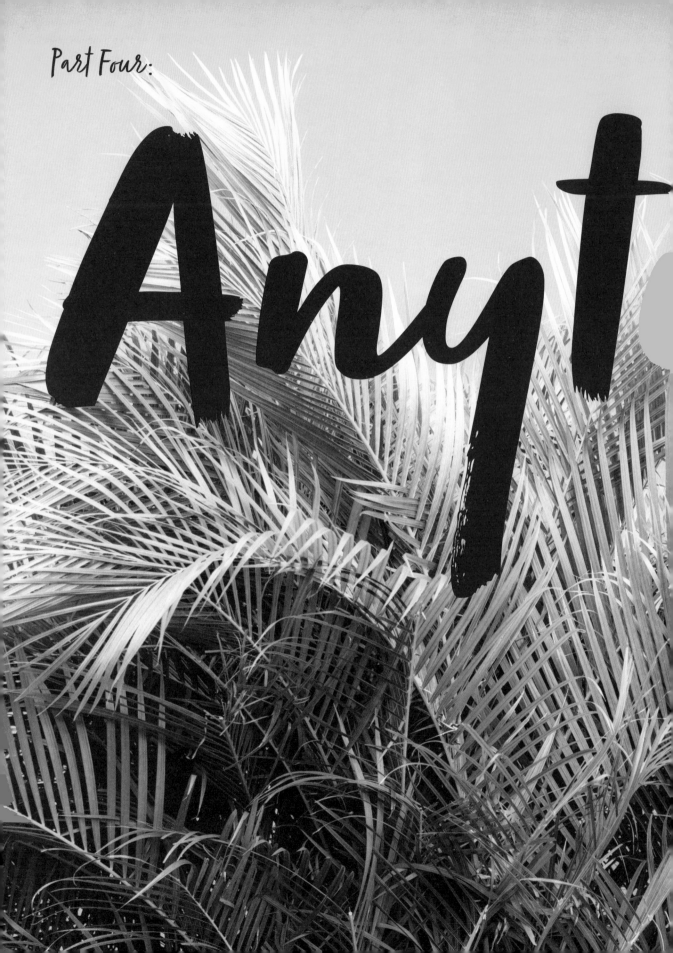

Part Four:

Anyt

Salted
Cashew
Brittle

Sugar High

Sugar High PLATTER

This candy platter is perfect for birthday parties, Halloween events, or anytime you want to give your guests an extra-sweet treat.

 STRATEGY: Seek out a candy shop that lets you purchase by the pound. Buying in bulk instead of in prepackaged bags will give you more variety. Try to stick to crowd pleasers while also selecting a variety of colors, flavors, and shapes.

You'll need a candy thermometer for the brittle recipe, as the mixture will need to come to 300°F [150°C], or else it won't harden up.

 **DRINK PAIRING**: Make soda shop sodas: Buy a bottle of sparkling water and a few syrup varieties to make your own flavored sodas. A few of my favorites are cherry-lime, blackberry, and pineapple.

SERVES 20

2.5 lb [680 g] chocolate candies (such as peanut butter cups, malt balls, nonpareils, chocolate-covered pretzels, etc.)

2.5 lb [680 g] hard and gummy candy (such as gummy bears, Swedish fish, gumdrops, rock candy, etc.)

Salted Cashew Brittle (recipe follows)

Using a large serving platter, cluster the chocolate candies on one-third of the platter, hard and gummy candies onto another third, and cashew brittle on the remaining portion. Avoiding direct sunlight (we don't want the chocolate melting on us!), serve at room temperature.

Salted Cashew Brittle

SERVES 20 AS A BOARD COMPONENT

2 cups [400 g] sugar

½ cup [160 g] light corn syrup

½ cup [110 g] unsalted butter, cubed

½ cup [120 ml] water

½ tsp baking soda

1½ cups [210 g] whole roasted cashews

Coarse sea salt

Line a baking sheet with parchment paper and butter the paper.

Add the sugar, corn syrup, butter, and water to a medium saucepan over medium-high heat. Whisk until the butter has melted and everything is combined.

Once the mixture begins simmering, stop whisking and let boil undisturbed until the temperature reaches 300°F [150°C], 10 to 12 minutes.

Once at 300°F [150°C], remove from the heat and quickly whisk in the baking soda and cashews.

Quickly pour onto the prepared baking sheet. Use a spatula to spread the mixture into an even layer. Let cool completely, about 1 hour, before breaking into at least twenty pieces.

Store leftover brittle in an airtight container with wax paper between the pieces (to prevent clumping) on the counter or in a dry location. Should last up to 3 weeks.

Flower
Power

Quick Rose-
Pickled Grapes

Flower Power PLATTER

My favorite part about this board is that it varies based on what flowers are in season, and it's the perfect way to add color to an appetizer table. The quick-pickled grapes have such a unique flavor; you first taste the tangy brine, but it's quickly complemented by the burst of the grape's sweet filling.

 STRATEGY : Give the board a bright and stunning look by using fresh-picked flowers, or evoke a moody feel with a bouquet of dried flowers.

I chop the goat cheese up with dried lavender and rose petals for an extra layer of texture, but you could also fold it into chèvre if you'd rather create a dip.

 DRINK PAIRING: Make a batch of elderflower gin and tonics. My go-to on hot summer evenings, a gin and tonic is so light and refreshing that it goes with anything. The floral tones of elderflower liqueur will have your guests smitten. To make six, mix 10 oz [300 ml] gin, 24 oz [720 ml] tonic water, and 6 oz [180 ml] elderflower liquor in a pitcher. Transfer to six cocktail glasses filled with ice and garnish with lemon slices.

WYATT'S MEATY SUGGESTION: Make prosciutto rosettes by twisting each piece into a long strand and wrapping it tightly around itself. If you have issues with it unraveling, tuck the end underneath.

SERVES 6 AS AN APPETIZER

- **6 oz [170 g] goat cheese (or chèvre)**
- **1 tsp culinary-grade dried lavender**
- **1 tsp culinary-grade dried rose petals or dried hibiscus**
- **3 oz [80 g] Parmesan cheese**
- **3 oz [85 g] blue cheese (such as Gorgonzola or blue Stilton)**
- **½ cup [170 g] wildflower honey**
- **Quick Rose-Pickled Grapes (recipe follows)**
- **Candied Pistachios (page 214) or 1½ cups [180 g] shelled lightly salted pistachios**
- **1 large baguette, sliced, or Quick Crostini (page 198)**
- **Smoked Gouda Cheese Straws (page 202) or 18 store-bought breadsticks**

Transfer the goat cheese to a cutting board and top with dried lavender and rose petals. Use a large knife to cut the dried flowers into the goat cheese until the flowers are incorporated and the goat cheese is cut into small pieces. Transfer to a shallow dish and place on your serving board. Add the Parmesan and blue cheese wedges to the serving board. Transfer the honey and pickled grapes (along with some of the pickling juice) to separate serving dishes and place on the serving board with serving spoons. Fill the board in with candied pistachios, baguette slices, and cheese straws.

Place wildflowers or a bouquet in a vase and display next to the board, if desired.

Quick Rose-Pickled Grapes

SERVES 6 AS A BOARD COMPONENT

8 oz [230 g] seedless grapes

¾ cup [180 ml] red wine vinegar

¾ cup [180 ml] water

5 peppercorns

1 small dried bay leaf

2 Tbsp sugar

1 Tbsp culinary-grade dried rose petals

1 Tbsp fine sea salt

Put the grapes into a clean and dry 1-pt [16-oz] Mason jar.

In a large saucepan, combine the vinegar, water, peppercorns, bay leaf, sugar, rose petals, and salt. Bring to a boil over high heat. Let boil for 1 minute, stirring to dissolve the sugar and salt. Remove from the heat and let cool for 5 minutes.

Strain the brine into the Mason jar, making sure it covers the grapes completely. Cover and refrigerate overnight or up to 1 week.

Medite

The Simplest
Red Wine
Sangria

ranean

Mediterranean

PLATTER

This Mediterranean-themed platter is perfect for a starter at your next gathering or as an easy dinner for two. We serve this light platter in the hot summer when cool hummus and sparkling sangria taste extra refreshing.

STRATEGY: Hummus is an ideal building block for a healthy and simple platter since it's loaded with protein and pairs well with most vegetables. It's easy to make your own at home, or your local grocery store may offer house-made verions with a variety of delicious flavors. I like to stick to a nonflavored hummus when serving a crowd, but sometimes Wyatt and I venture into buying a roasted garlic or spicy version if enjoying it as a dinner for two.

DRINK PAIRING: Serve it with The Simplest Red Wine Sangria (recipe follows), subtly sweetened with orange juice.

WYATT'S MEATY SUGGESTION: Add a Mediterranean cured sausage such as mortadella to keep in tandem with the theme of this board.

SERVES 6 AS AN APPETIZER

1 cup [450 g] hummus

¾ cup [100 g] olives

1½ cups [500 g] marinated peppers (I stuffed mine with mozzarella balls) or roasted peppers

6 oz [170 g] pita slices

6 oz [170 g] mozzarella balls

¾ cup [105 g] mixed nuts

3 cups [480 g] red seedless grapes

Olive oil, for garnish

Basil, for garnish

Freshly ground black pepper

Spread the hummus in the center of a large platter. Scatter the olives, peppers, pita slices, mozzarella, nuts, and grapes around the hummus. Drizzle olive oil over the hummus and sprinkle with basil and pepper.

The Simplest
Red Wine Sangria

SERVES 6

1 orange, sliced

1 lemon, sliced

1 lime, sliced

1 bottle [750 ml] red wine
(such as Merlot, Cabernet
Sauvignon, or Shiraz)

½ cup [120 ml] Triple Sec

1 cup [240 ml] orange juice

1½ cups [360 ml] soda water

Ice

Add orange slices, lemon slices, and lime slices to a large pitcher. Pour in the red wine, Triple Sec, orange juice, and soda water. Add ice and serve.

Miniature
Cali Skewers

California Dre

California Dreaming BOARD

This platter will allow you to pretend you're at a swanky California party. I was obsessed with the show *The O.C.* which in turn became an obsession with California and throwing fancy parties like the "Newpsies" on the show (insert *90210*, *Laguna Beach*, and/or *Baywatch* joke here if that was more your thing).

STRATEGY: Look for artisanal Californian companies when buying your food for this board to keep with the theme. I was first introduced to Cypress Grove's legendary Humboldt Fog cheese when traveling the West Coast and would recommend seeking it out for this board—I later found it in my tiny Indiana town, so I bet you can, too!

DRINK PAIRING: Serve with your favorite Californian dry white wine.

WYATT'S MEATY SUGGESTION: Serve with a batch of California cured lean bison jerky.

SERVES 12

Miniature Cali Skewers (recipe follows)

6 oz [170 g] Humboldt Fog cheese or another iconic California cheese

6 oz [170 g] hard or crumbled cheese from California

¼ cup [85 g] honey

8 oz [230 g] assorted brine-cured olives

1½ cups [210 g] whole raw almonds

8 oz [230 g] crackers

8 slices multigrain bread, cut into 6 pieces each

1 cup [160 g] California-grown grapes

12 fresh figs

Add the skewers and their dressing to one side of the serving board. Put the Humboldt Fog cheese on a small serving dish and add to the board. Place the other cheese on the opposite side of board. Transfer the honey and olives to small dishes and place on the board with serving spoons. Fill in the remaining space with almonds, crackers, bread, grapes, and figs.

Miniature Cali Skewers

SERVES 12 AS A BOARD COMPONENT

Dressing:

1 cup [240 g] sour cream

¼ cup [60 ml] buttermilk

1 garlic clove, minced

1 Tbsp freshly squeezed lemon juice

1 tsp fine sea salt

Freshly ground black pepper

1 Tbsp olive oil

Skewers:

4 slices multigrain bread, cut into 6 pieces each, toasted

12 cherry tomatoes

1 avocado, flesh cut into 12 cubes

½ cup [30 g] alfalfa sprouts

12 slices of Colby or Monterey Jack cheese, cut into 4 squares each

To make the dressing, in a small bowl, whisk together the sour cream, buttermilk, garlic, lemon juice, salt, and pepper. While whisking, slowly pour in the olive oil and whisk until emulsified. Transfer to a small serving bowl, cover, and let chill in the refrigerator for at least 30 minutes.

To make the skewers, thread a piece of bread onto a wooden skewer, followed by a cherry tomato, avocado cube, sprouts, a folded cheese slice, and another piece of bread. Repeat with the rest of the bread, tomatoes, avocado, sprouts, and cheese to make 12 skewers.

Serve alongside the buttermilk dressing with a small spoon so guests can scoop the dressing over their skewer before enjoying. Store leftover dressing in an airtight container in the refrigerator for up to 5 days.

Southern

Pimiento Dip

Southern-Style BOARD

Celebrate the South with this comforting board. I still remember Wyatt's excitement the first time I made him a batch of Pimiento Dip. It is one of the few foods I've watched him devour in one sitting. Now he's the one who whips up a batch to munch on with crackers.

STRATEGY: Go on a hunt for cheeses made in the American South. They aren't available in the same abundance as European cheeses, but you'll be able to find some at your local cheese shop, and you may just discover your new favorite cheese. A few southern farms to look up with big cheese selections are Sweet Home Farm in Alabama, Mountain View Farm in Virginia, Sweet Grass Dairy in Georgia, and Chapel Hill Creamery in North Carolina.

DRINK PAIRING: No southern gathering would be complete without a big pitcher of sweet tea!

WYATT'S MEATY SUGGESTION: Serve with country-cured ham, a dry-cured meat originally hailing from rural parts of the southeastern United States. It can be mail-ordered or found at many good deli or meat counters.

SERVES 6

8 oz [230 g] cream cheese

2 Tbsp red pepper jam

6 oz [170 g] hard or semisoft cheese from the American South

6 oz [170 g] soft cheese from the American South

Pimiento Dip (recipe follows)

6 Tbsp [120 g] peach jam

6 Tbsp [90 g] Whole-Grain Ale Mustard (page 209) or store-bought whole-grain mustard

¾ cup [120 g] pecans

¾ cup [120 g] peanuts

2 large oranges, peeled and segmented

2 peaches, sliced

4 oz [115 g] crackers

Put the cream cheese on a plate, pour the red pepper jam over it, and put it in the center of the board. Place the other two cheeses on opposite sides of the board with cheese knives. Place the Pimiento Dip, peach jam, and mustard in individual bowls and add to the board with serving spoons in each. Fill in the remaining space with pecans, peanuts, orange slices, peach slices, and crackers.

Pimiento Dip

SERVES 6 AS A BOARD COMPONENT

2 cups [160 g] grated Cheddar cheese

½ cup [120 g] mayonnaise

2 Tbsp sour cream

2 Tbsp store-bought diced pimientos

2 tsp pickle relish

Fine sea salt

Freshly ground black pepper

Hot sauce

In a medium bowl, use a fork to mix together the cheese, mayonnaise, sour cream, pimientos, and relish. Season with salt, pepper, and hot sauce.

Cover and let chill in the refrigerator for at least 30 minutes. To store, transfer to an airtight container and keep in the refrigerator for up to 5 days.

Hazelnut
Hot Fudge

Sun

Sundae SPREAD

A sundae station is my go-to build-your-own party spread because it appeals to folks of all ages. Also, if you'd like to make the whole event collaborative, ask your guests to each bring a topping so you end up with diverse mix-ins that you may not have thought of!

STRATEGY: Since the mix-ins are the main show here, offer ice creams that don't already have swirls or mix-ins in them, to allow guests to customize their sundaes with the toppings of their choice. I like to use two basic flavors for the ice cream base, such as chocolate and vanilla, and then one slightly more exotic flavor, such as strawberry or caramel. To customize this spread to however many folks you are serving, plan to have 1½ cups [12 oz] of ice cream, 4 to 5 Tbsp of toppings, and 3 to 4 Tbsp of syrup, jam, or whipped cream for each person (that is generous, but you don't want to run out!). Also, make sure you have enough bowls, and lots of ice on hand to fill the buckets of ice cream. Ask your friends or neighbors if you can borrow an ice cream scoop so you have at least one for each flavor of ice cream.

DRINK PAIRING: Ice cream can make people thirsty. Have a pitcher of iced tea or ice water nearby for guests to enjoy.

SERVES 20

5 pt [2.4 L] vanilla bean ice cream

5 pt [2.4 L] chocolate ice cream

5 pt [2.4 L] ice cream in a third flavor without mix-ins (such as strawberry, caramel, coffee, etc.)

1 cup [140 to 180 g] bite-size fruits (such as berries, maraschino cherries, banana slices, etc.)

1 cup [180 g] chocolate pieces (such as chocolate chips, M&M's, chocolate-covered coffee beans, crushed Oreos, etc.)

1 cup [200 g] candy sprinkles

½ cup [40 g] coconut flakes, toasted

½ cup [60 g] Granola Two Ways (page 49) or store-bought granola

½ cup [55 g] chopped nuts (such as slivered almonds, pecan pieces, etc.) or trail mix

½ cup [45 g] crushed potato chips or pretzels

½ cup [150 g] candy (such as gummy bears, toffee bits, etc.)

½ cup [60 g] cereal

½ cup [150 g] jam

Hazelnut Hot Fudge (recipe follows)

1 cup [330 g] caramel sauce

1 cup [40 g] whipped cream

Fill several coolers or ice buckets with ice and place the containers of ice cream in them. Transfer all the toppings to small dishes and place little serving spoons in each dish. Place bowls on the side of the table where guests will begin making their sundaes. Next to the bowls, add the ice cream buckets and then add the bowls of toppings, with the bowls of jam, fudge, caramel, and whipped cream at the far end of the table.

If setting up the table in advance, place everything in its spot except the ice and ice cream. Add ice and ice cream right before your guests arrive.

Hazelnut Hot Fudge

SERVES 20 AS A SPREAD COMPONENT

6 oz [170 g] bittersweet chocolate, finely chopped

⅔ cup [160 ml] heavy cream

½ cup [160 g] light corn syrup

¼ cup [45 g] lightly packed brown sugar

¼ cup [25 g] Dutch-process cocoa powder

½ tsp fine sea salt

2 Tbsp unsalted butter

¼ cup [70 g] Nutella hazelnut spread

In a medium saucepan over medium-low heat, whisk half of the chocolate, the heavy cream, corn syrup, brown sugar, cocoa powder, and salt until combined. Bring to a boil and maintain at a low boil for 5 minutes, stirring often. Remove from the heat and stir in the butter, the other half of the chocolate, and Nutella until smooth. Serve warm.

Deviled
Eggs

Basic

Beet-Pickled

Crème
Fraîche

Deviled Egg PLATTER

This platter features three versions of deviled eggs. The eggs are surrounded by garnish options for even more variations for your guests to experiment with.

STRATEGY: Start on the Beet-Pickled Deviled Eggs at least a day before your party, as they need to sit in the pickle juice for at least 12 hours. Note that the longer they are in the beet juice, the deeper pink their rims will be but the tougher the egg white gets. (Some people love this tough texture, but I personally am not a fan. The right amount for my taste is 14 to 16 hours of pickling.) Consider topping a few eggs with garnish to inspire your guests and so they know how the platter is intended to be used.

DRINK PAIRING: Serve with something that won't overpower the eggs. My suggestion is a gin sour (which consists of only gin, lemon juice, and simple syrup) or a simple martini.

WYATT'S MEATY SUGGESTION: If looking to add meat to your platter, top deviled eggs with smoked salmon, a cured delicacy known for pairing well with eggs.

SERVES 8

8 Basic Deviled Eggs (recipe follows)

8 Crème Fraîche Deviled Eggs (recipe follows)

8 Beet-Pickled Deviled Eggs (recipe follows)

2 small pickled beets, cut into matchsticks

2 Tbsp chopped fresh chives

2 Tbsp chopped fresh parsley

2 small radishes, cut into matchsticks (quick-pickle them in leftover beet juice from the beet pickles for an extra-tangy topping!)

2 Tbsp crumbled blue cheese

2 Tbsp chopped fresh dill

¼ cup [60 g] pickled jalapeños

2 to 3 Tbsp hot sauce

2 Tbsp chopped pitted black olives

¼ cup [40 g] quartered cherry tomatoes

2 Tbsp white or black sesame seeds

2 Tbsp capers

Spread out the deviled eggs evenly around board. Place the remaining ingredients in individual pinch dishes with serving spoons and forks, and place either on the deviled egg platter (if there is room) or on a platter right next to the deviled eggs. Serve right away.

Basic Deviled Eggs

MAKES 8 DEVILED EGGS

4 eggs

¼ cup [60 g] mayonnaise

1 tsp yellow mustard

1 tsp sweet relish

Dash of fine sea salt

Dash of freshly ground black pepper

Paprika, for sprinkling

Place the eggs in a single layer in a saucepan and add enough water to cover by at least 1½ in [4 cm]. Heat on high until boiling. Let boil 1 minute, remove from the heat, cover, and let sit for 12 minutes. Drain and run the eggs under cold water for 1 minute. Crack the shells and carefully peel the eggs (I usually do this under cold running water for best results).

Slice the eggs in half lengthwise. Scoop out the egg yolks and put them in a small bowl. Set aside the egg whites. Add the mayonnaise, mustard, and relish to the bowl with the egg yolks and use a fork to mash them together until combined. Season with salt and pepper. Divide the filling evenly between the egg whites using either a small spoon or piping bag. Sprinkle with paprika. Serve immediately.

Crème Fraîche Deviled Eggs

MAKES 8 DEVILED EGGS

4 eggs

¼ cup [60 g] crème fraîche

2 Tbsp mayonnaise

1 tsp Dijon mustard

1 tsp white wine vinegar

Dash of fine sea salt

Dash of freshly ground black pepper

Place the eggs in a single layer in a saucepan and add enough water to cover by at least 1½ in [4 cm]. Heat on high until boiling. Let boil 1 minute, remove from the heat, cover, and let sit for 12 minutes. Drain and run the eggs under cold water for 1 minute. Crack the shells and carefully peel the eggs (I usually do this under cold running water for best results).

Slice the eggs in half lengthwise. Scoop out the egg yolks and put them in a small bowl. Set aside the egg whites. Add the crème fraîche, mayonnaise, mustard, and vinegar to the bowl with the egg yolks and use a fork to mash them together until combined. Season with salt and pepper. Divide the filling evenly between the egg whites using either a small spoon or piping bag. Serve immediately.

Beet-Pickled Deviled Eggs

MAKES 8 DEVILED EGGS

4 eggs

One 16-oz [455-g] jar of pickled beets

½ cup [120 ml] white wine vinegar

2 Tbsp lightly packed brown sugar

1 Tbsp pink peppercorns + freshly ground pink peppercorns

1 tsp fine sea salt + more for seasoning

¼ cup [60 g] mayonnaise

1 tsp yellow mustard

1 tsp sweet relish

Place the eggs in a single layer in a saucepan and add enough water to cover by at least 1½ in [4 cm]. Heat on high until boiling. Let boil 1 minute, remove from the heat, cover, and let sit for 12 minutes. Drain and run the eggs under cold water for 1 minute. Crack the shells and carefully peel the eggs (I usually do this under cold running water for best results).

Place the eggs in a large Mason jar. Pour the pickled beets and their juices, the vinegar, brown sugar, peppercorns, and salt over the eggs. Cover and gently shake to make sure everything is mixed together. Refrigerate for 14 to 16 hours (longer if you want a deeper pink rim, but the egg whites will be tougher the longer they pickle).

Using a slotted spoon, remove the eggs from the pickle mixture. Slice all the eggs in half lengthwise. Scoop out the egg yolks and put them in a small bowl. Set aside the egg whites. Add the mayonnaise, mustard, and relish to the bowl with the egg yolks and use a fork to mash them together until combined. Season with salt and ground pink pepper. Divide the filling evenly between the egg whites using either a small spoon or piping bag.

Chop two pickled beets into matchsticks pieces and put in a pinch dish on the garnish tray. Serve immediately.

Caprese

GARLIC CONFIT

Caprese PLATTER

Caprese is an Italian salad consisting of fresh mozzarella, tomatoes, and basil; this board features those simple three ingredients in an array of variations.

STRATEGY: Cut the mozzarella into a variety of shapes and choose tomatoes in a mix of colors and sizes to create a stunning display.

DRINK PAIRING: It's tomato season, which means it's hot as all get-out, so stick to some crisp chilled white wine like Pinot Bianco.

WYATT'S MEATY SUGGESTION: Unlike a lot of seafood, tilapia does not have an overbearing fishy smell and so may appeal even to those who don't typically like fish. Preparing this fish is as simple as placing the fillets on a baking sheet, seasoning with salt and pepper, and baking at 425°F [220°C] for 10 to 15 minutes, or until opaque throughout. Your end result will be a light and flaky fillet.

SERVES 24 AS AN APPETIZER (1 OZ PER GUEST)

Garlic Confit (recipe follows)

10 oz [285 g] cherry tomatoes

4 large heirloom tomatoes, sliced ¼ in [6 mm] thick

8 oz [230 g] fresh mozzarella balls, small

8 oz [230 g] fresh mozzarella ball, cut into 8 slices

8 oz [230 g] Burrata cheese

24 baguette slices, toasted, or Quick Crostini (page 198)

1 cup [12 g / 40 to 50 leaves] loosely packed fresh green and/or purple basil leaves

Microgreens, for garnish (optional)

Transfer the Garlic Confit to a clean serving bowl. Cut half of the cherry tomatoes in half, leaving the other half of them whole. Arrange a large cheeseboard with the garlic confit, halved and whole cherry tomatoes, the heirloom tomatoes, mozzarella, Burrata, baguette slices, and basil. Sprinkle the microgreens (if using) over the tomatoes. Serve right away.

Garlic Confit

SERVES 24 AS A BOARD COMPONENT

2 heads garlic (about 26 cloves), peeled

5 sprigs fresh rosemary

1 dried bay leaf

1 cup [240 ml] olive oil

In a small saucepan, combine the peeled garlic cloves, rosemary, and bay leaf and top with olive oil. Cook over medium-low heat for 1 hour, or until the garlic is tender. Remove and discard the rosemary and bay leaf.

Let cool to room temperature and transfer to a sterile jar.

Serve by scooping out garlic cloves and smashing them onto a piece of toast with mozzarella and tomatoes.

NOTE: Due to bacteria being able to build up, it's important that you store any garlic confit leftovers in a sterile airtight jar with the garlic completely covered in olive oil; it should last up to 4 days in the refrigerator. Alternatively, you can put two or three garlic cloves into each well of an ice-cube tray, cover them with the remaining olive oil, and put in the freezer. When the garlic confit cubes are frozen, transfer them to a freezer bag and store them in the freezer for up to 3 months.

Lemon-Herb
White Bean Dip

Veg Out! PLATTER

This platter full of crudités with easy dips and spreads is a fool-proof appetizer assortment for when you are having a casual gathering.

STRATEGY: Pick out your favorite raw vegetables for this platter, keeping in mind a mix of shapes and sizes. I'd suggest heading to your farmers' market to guarantee a variety of the freshest vegetables.

DRINK PAIRING: Serve refreshing mint Mojitos to complement all the fresh veggies in this platter.

WYATT'S MEATY SUGGESTION: If you are enjoying this platter near the coast, head to a nearby fish market to pick up some oysters for a light and fresh companion.

SERVES 12 AS AN APPETIZER

Blueberry Thyme Compound Butter (page 217), chilled and sliced

Lemon-Herb White Bean dip (recipe follows)

Marinated Feta with Sun-Dried Tomato, Thyme, and Garlic (page 206)

12 cups [1.92 kg] raw vegetables (such as radishes, cherry tomatoes, celery sticks, carrots, bell pepper strips, broccoli florets, cauliflower florets, snap peas, endive, etc.)

Lay the slices of compound butter on a small serving dish. Add the butter dish, white bean dip, and marinated feta onto the serving platter, leaving plenty of space between them. Fill in the remaining space with raw vegetables.

Lemon-Herb White Bean Dip

**SERVES 12 AS A BOARD COMPONENT,
OR 6 ON ITS OWN**

**Two 15.5-oz [445-g] cans cannellini
beans, rinsed and drained**

**3 Tbsp [45 ml] olive oil + more for
garnish**

**2 tsp torn fresh basil leaves + more
for garnish**

**2 tsp fresh thyme leaves + more for
garnish**

2 tsp fresh rosemary leaves

2 Tbsp freshly squeezed lemon juice

½ tsp fresh lemon zest

½ tsp fine sea salt

Dash of freshly ground black pepper

¼ cup [60 ml] water

Microgreens, for garnish (optional)

In a food processor, pulse the cannellini beans, olive oil, basil, thyme, rosemary, lemon juice and zest, salt, and pepper until combined, about 30 seconds. With the food processor running, slowly add the water and continue to process until smooth, about 30 seconds more. Transfer to a serving bowl and garnish with more olive oil, microgreens (if using), and herbs.

Triple Cheese
Truffle Oil Fo

Fondue

Fondue SPREAD

Fondue (the French word for "melt") was a popular party theme in the fifties, sixties, and seventies in the United States, and it's still just as thrilling to have a fondue party today as it was back then! With little preparation required and a communal serving style, fondue is an interactive way to bring people together at the table.

STRATEGY: Dice and prepare as much of the food ahead of time as you can. Steam the vegetables and cook the fondue right before eating. Look for color-coded fondue spears so that each guest can keep track of their own eating utensils (especially if guests are eating directly from the spears instead of transferring to their plates and using forks).

DRINK PAIRING: Serve with an aromatic white wine like a Riesling. If you want to serve something more unique, add a splash of Kirsch, a German cherry brandy, as it is traditionally added to many cheese fondue recipes.

WYATT'S MEATY SUGGESTION: Salami and cheese are already a delicious match, but when this salty meat is dipped in warm fondue, it reaches an entirely new level of mouthwatering.

SERVES 6

Triple Cheese Truffle Oil Fondue (recipe follows)
1 head broccoli, chopped into florets
6 medium carrots, peeled and diced
1 head cauliflower, chopped into florets
2 bell peppers, cut into strips
2 cups [170 g] snap peas
3 apples, chopped into bite-size pieces
2 tsp freshly squeezed lemon juice
3 cups [480 g] seedless grapes
1 pumpernickel loaf, cut into bite-size pieces
1 French bread loaf, cut into bite-size pieces

Transfer the fondue to a fondue pot and place in the center of your serving table.

Working in batches, lightly steam the broccoli, carrots, cauliflower, and bell peppers. Transfer the veggies to a platter with the snap peas and set on the serving table. Lightly toss the apple slices in lemon juice, place on a plate with the grapes, and put on the serving table.

Combine the two breads on the last plate and place on the serving table.

Triple Cheese Truffle Oil Fondue

MAKES 1½ CUPS [400 G]

1 garlic clove, halved

1 tsp olive oil

2 tsp cornstarch

1 cup [240 ml] dry white wine

1½ cups [110 g] shredded white Cheddar cheese

1½ cups [110 g] shredded Gruyère or Swiss cheese

1 cup [80 g] shredded Emmental cheese

Freshly ground black pepper

1½ tsp white truffle oil

Rub the garlic all over the inside of a medium saucepan set over medium-low heat. Add the olive oil and cornstarch and whisk together. Slowly pour in the white wine while whisking. Turn the heat to medium and let cook until simmering. Once simmering, add small handfuls of the shredded cheeses to the mixture, constantly whisking and making sure the cheese has completely melted before adding another handful. Once all the cheese has been added and melted, remove from the heat and season with pepper.

Transfer the fondue to a fondue pot and drizzle with truffle oil. Serve right away.

Pickle

Bread and Butter
Pickled Vegetables

Pickle PLATTER

Move over cheese, we have a new star in town: pickles! With all the components of a standard cheeseboard, this platter emphasizes an array of tangy pickled vegetables with just a little sprinkle of cheese and condiments.

STRATEGY: Source out local pickle brands for this board—you may be surprised to find unique types of pickles that are being made in your neck of the woods. Don't be afraid to swap in those unusual kinds for any of the types listed in the recipe. Also, prep your homemade Bread and Butter Pickled Vegetables at least 1 day ahead of time. You'll need three 1-pt [16-oz] Mason jars for the recipe.

DRINK PAIRING: Pick a sweet rosé wine to help counter the acidity of this board.

WYATT'S MEATY SUGGESTION: Seek out an array of salty cured sausages, which will work well with the tangy pickles.

SERVES 32 AS AN APPETIZER

Bread and Butter Pickled Vegetables (recipe follows)

One 16-oz [455-g] jar pickled beets

One 14.5-oz [440-g] jar pickled jalapeño slices

One 15-oz [430-g] jar pickled asparagus or okra

One 14-oz [400-g] jar cornichons

One 16-oz [473-ml] jar giardiniera pickled vegetable mix

Quick Rose-Pickled Grapes (page 146) or another store-bought pickled fruit

2 cups [480 g] Whole-Grain Ale Mustard (page 209) or store-bought whole-grain mustard

Smoked Gouda Cheese Straws (page 202) or store-bought cheese straws

Two 8-oz [230-g] wedges or balls soft cheese (such as Camembert or mozzarella)

32 oz [960 g] crackers

Place all the pickles and the mustard into individual dishes and transfer onto a serving tray. On a separate tray or board nearby, place the cheese straws, cheese, and crackers. Insert small spoons or tongs into each pickle and mustard bowl and place near the cheese. Serve immediately.

Bread and Butter Pickled Vegetables

MAKES 3 PT [850 G]

- **2 cups [480 ml] white vinegar**
- **2 cups [480 ml] water**
- **½ cup [100 g] sugar**
- **1 Tbsp fine sea salt**
- **1 tsp mustard seeds**
- **½ tsp celery seeds**
- **3 medium carrots, cut into 3-in [7.5-cm] chunks**
- **1 bell pepper, cut into 3-in [7.5-cm] strips**
- **1 cucumber, sliced crosswise**
- **1 bunch radishes, sliced**

In a small saucepan, combine the vinegar, water, sugar, salt, mustard seeds, and celery seeds. Bring to a boil over medium-high heat and let boil for 1 minute, stirring often, or until the sugar and salt dissolve.

Divide the vegetables between three sterile and dry 1-pt [16-oz] Mason jars, and pour the hot vinegar mixture into each jar, making sure all the vegetables are completely submerged. Cover and let sit on the counter to cool for at least 1 hour.

Transfer the pickle jars to the refrigerator and let chill overnight. Store in the refrigerator for up to 2 weeks.

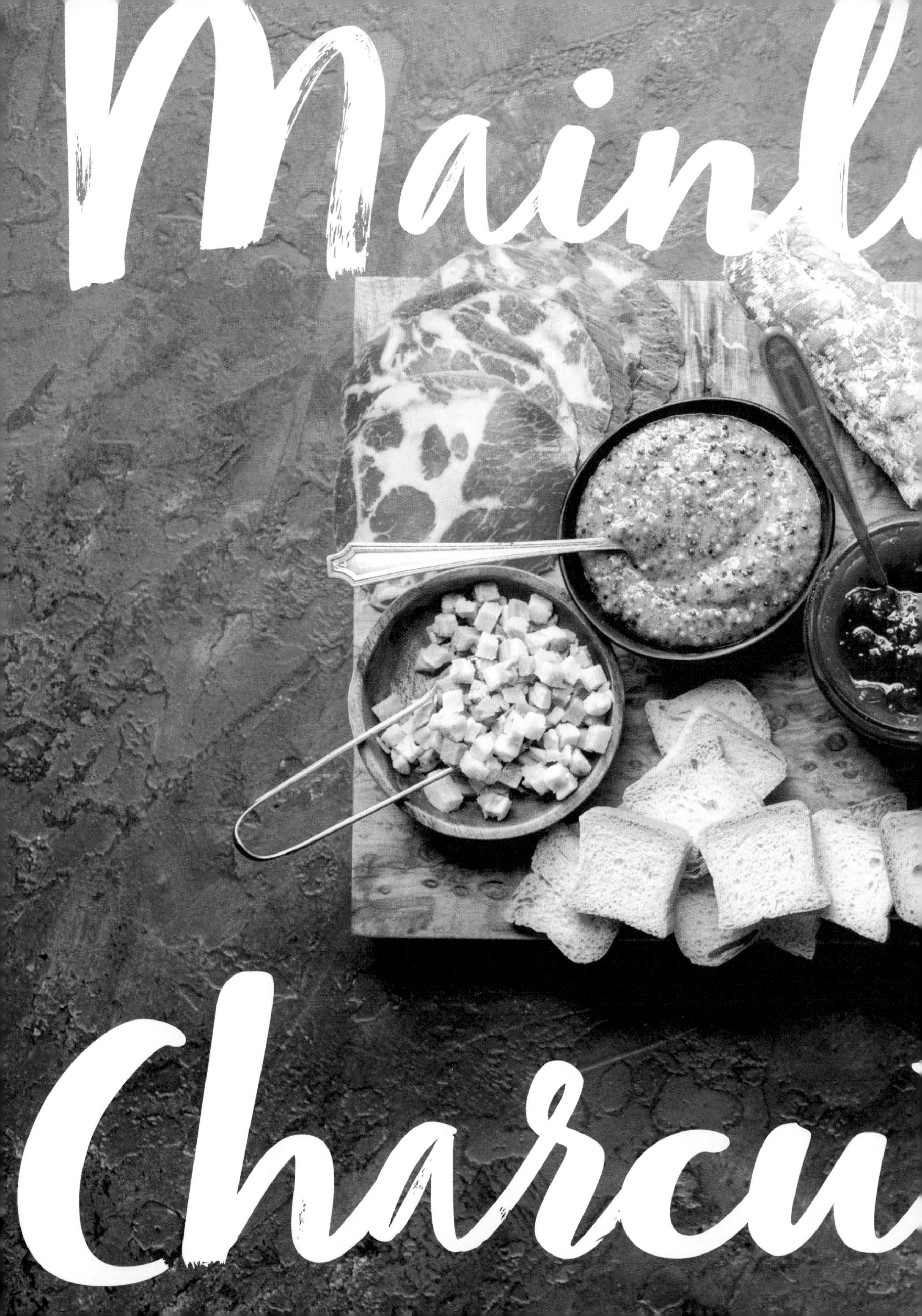
Mainl
Charcu

Meat

Hot Honey

erie

Mainly Meat Charcuterie

BOARD BY WYATT

Mix up your appetizer game by swapping in this low-maintenance and crowd-pleasing arrangement. This is a great way to introduce your guests to specialty cured meats they may have never ventured to try before.

STRATEGY: Mix up the textures by adding thinly sliced, diced, and marbled meats. Serve with cornichons (tiny pickles) as a palate cleanser between bites.

DRINK PAIRING: An excellent lager beer balances out the saltiness of the cured meats by providing a cool, smooth, and carbonated finish.

SHELLY'S VEGGIE SUGGESTION: Swap the cornichons for a batch of Quick-Pickled Vegetables (page 63). They still make great palate cleansers and give a little more variety to this meaty board.

SERVES 8 AS AN APPETIZER

- 8 tsp [40 g] **Whole-Grain Ale Mustard (page 209) or store-bought whole-grain mustard**
- ½ cup [160 g] **cherry jam**
- 8 oz [230 g] **cornichons**
- **Hot Honey (recipe follows)**
- 4 oz [115 g] **prosciutto**
- 4 oz [115 g] **capocollo**
- 8 oz [230 g] **sopressata salami**
- 4 oz [115 g] **cubed cooked pancetta**
- 8 oz [230 g] **toast or crackers**

Place the mustard, jam, pickles, and hot honey in small bowls and group in the middle of the board. Roll up each piece of prosciutto and place on the board. Place the remaining meats around the board to fill it out, keeping the meats from touching, if possible.

Hot Honey

MAKES ⅓ CUP [110 G] HONEY

⅓ cup [110 g] honey

1½ tsp red pepper flakes

Combine the honey and red pepper flakes in a small saucepan over medium heat. Let warm until the honey just begins to simmer. Remove from heat and let steep for at least 30 minutes. Strain out most of the red pepper flakes using a fine-mesh sieve (leaving a few remaining if you like it extra spicy).

Clean Out
Your Pantry

White Wine–Warmed Olives
with Orange and Rosemary

Clean Out Your Pantry SMORGASBORD

Whip up this board with any leftover odds and ends you have in your refrigerator or pantry. See pages 18 to 22 for more suggestions of what to use. Hummus or dips will also make great additions to this dish if they are already in your refrigerator.

STRATEGY: Jazz up store-bought olives with this simple white wine marinade (I can't be the only one who constantly has half bottles of wine in my refrigerator, right?). Use your favorite olives; I like to pick out a variety of shapes and colors for a pretty presentation. Choose a quality white wine as it won't be cooked off and the flavor will be prominent; I prefer a dry wine with the tiniest hint of sweet (Sauvignon Blanc or Chardonnay are good choices) as it complements the savory rosemary and briny olives beautifully.

DRINK PAIRING: Finish off that bottle of white wine you used for the warmed olives.

WYATT'S MEATY SUGGESTION: Have some leftover deli meat slices from weekday lunches? Add them to your board to enjoy with the crackers and cheese.

SERVES 2 AS A MAIN

White Wine–Warmed Olives with Orange and Rosemary (recipe follows)

2 oz [55 g] soft or semisoft cheese (such as Camembert or goat cheese)

2 oz [55 g] hard cheese (such as Parmesan or Gouda)

2 Tbsp jam or jelly (such as cherry or blueberry)

2 Tbsp honey

4 Tbsp [40 g] mixed nuts (roasted or raw)

1 cup [140 to 160 g] fruit (such as grapes, chopped apples, or berries)

1 cup [60 to 140 g] chopped raw or marinated vegetables (such as carrots, bell pepper slices, tomatoes, etc.)

2 oz [55 g] crackers or ½ sliced baguette

Place the warmed olives and cheeses on individual plates and add to the table. Place the jam, honey, and nuts in individual bowls and add to the table. Add serving spoons and cheese knives. Fill in the remaining space with fruit, vegetables, and crackers. Serve right away.

White Wine-Warmed Olives with Orange and Rosemary

SERVES 2 AS A MAIN OR 4 AS AN APPETIZER

¼ cup [60 ml] olive oil

1 garlic clove

1 tsp peppercorns

One 6-in [15-cm] sprig fresh rosemary

Two 5-in [12-cm] strips orange zest

¼ cup [60 ml] white wine

8 oz [230 g] assorted brine-cured olives

Warm the olive oil, garlic clove, peppercorns, and rosemary sprig in a small saucepan or skillet over medium heat. Cook, stirring occasionally, until the garlic browns around the edges, 5 to 7 minutes. Turn the heat off (but keep the pan on the warm burner) and add the orange zest, white wine, and olives. Let sit for 15 minutes to marinate. Serve right away or store in an airtight container in the refrigerator for up to 3 days. Reheat before serving.

Part Five

Essen

tials

Quick Crostini

Use this recipe if you'd like to make your own crostini. Make sure you cut the baguette into slices ½ in [12 mm] thick, as thinner slices may get soggy and not hold toppings well and thicker slices will be more difficult to bite into. Also, use good-quality bread when making these, as the ingredients are so simple that the texture and flavor of the bread are essential.

MAKES ABOUT 50 PIECES

1 baguette

½ cup [120 ml] olive oil

1 tsp fine sea salt

½ tsp freshly ground black pepper

Raw garlic clove or peel of 1 fresh organic lemon (optional)

Preheat the oven to 350°F [180°C].

Cut the baguette into slices ½ in [12 mm] thick and transfer into a single layer on two large baking sheets. Brush both sides of the baguette slices with olive oil and sprinkle with salt and pepper. Bake for 15 minutes, or until golden brown, flipping the crostini halfway through and rotating the trays. When the crostini come out of the oven, rub with halved garlic or lemon peel for a subtle flavor, if desired.

Let cool before serving.

Store at room temperature in an airtight container or bag for up to 1 week.

Smoky Sweet Mixed Nuts

This subtly sweet nut mixture complements earthy cheeses (like blue-veined varieties) perfectly. Mix and match all your favorite nuts to create different combinations every time you make this. This recipe is also a perfect holiday gift for friends, since it keeps for 2 weeks at room temperature in an airtight container.

MAKES 2½ CUPS [320 G]

- **1 tsp smoked paprika**
- **1 tsp ground cinnamon**
- **½ tsp fine sea salt**
- **⅓ cup [60 g] lightly packed brown sugar**
- **1 egg white**
- **2 cups [280 g] mixed nuts (such as pecans, hazelnuts, cashews, peanuts, or macadamias)**

Preheat the oven to 300°F [150°C] and line a baking sheet with parchment paper.

In a small bowl, whisk together the smoked paprika, cinnamon, salt, and brown sugar.

In a large mixing bowl, whisk the egg white until frothy, about 20 seconds. Fold the mixed nuts into the egg white until completely coated. Sprinkle the spice mixture over the nuts and toss to coat.

Transfer the nuts to the prepared baking sheet and bake for 30 minutes, tossing every 10 minutes, until browned and fragrant.

Remove from the oven and let cool completely. Serve once cooled, or transfer to an airtight container and store at room temperature for up to 2 weeks.

Smoked Gouda Cheese Straws

Buttery Gouda replaces traditional Cheddar cheese in these savory cheese straws. Similar to a cheese cracker, these long and thin straws give a varied shape perfect for adding a new element to your cheeseboard. I like to display these fanning over the edge of the board for a dramatic effect.

MAKES ABOUT 60 STRAWS

8 oz [230 g] smoked Gouda, cut into large chunks

2 cups [240 g] all-purpose flour + more for flouring

½ tsp fine sea salt

½ tsp smoked paprika

½ tsp chili powder

¾ cup [165 g] cold unsalted butter, cubed

¼ cup [60 ml] whole milk

Place a rack in the middle of the oven and preheat to 350°F [180°C]. Line three baking sheets with parchment paper.

In a food processor, pulse the Gouda chunks for 15 seconds, or until the cheese is chopped into small pieces. Add the flour, salt, paprika, and chili powder and pulse three or four times, or until combined. Next, add the butter cubes and pulse for 30 seconds, or until a crumbly dough forms. With the food processor running, slowly pour in the milk and process until the dough forms into a large ball.

Taking a heaping 1-tsp [12-g] piece of dough, use both hands to roll it into an 8-in [20-cm] long cylinder on a clean surface. Transfer to a prepared baking sheet. Repeat with the rest of the dough to make 60 straws, putting 20 straws on each baking sheet.

Bake one tray at a time for 12 to 15 minutes, or until the straws start to brown (they will harden up as they cool, so don't be worried if they still look soft).

Transfer the cheese straws to a wire rack and let cool completely.

Repeat with the remaining two trays.

Store in an airtight container at room temperature for up to 5 days.

Homemade Seedy White Cheddar Crackers

These versatile crackers are great for enter-taining, as the dough can be made months in advance. The method for making the dough couldn't be easier since it's similar to making slice-and-bake cookies. If you already have the grater out for the cheese, go ahead and grate your cold butter, too—this is a tip I learned from a local pastry chef that helps the butter work into the dough much faster.

MAKES 35 CRACKERS

- ½ cup [60 g] all-purpose flour
- ½ cup [70 g] whole-wheat flour
- 1 cup [115 g] finely grated sharp Cheddar cheese
- 1 tsp + 2 Tbsp white sesame seeds
- ½ tsp + 1 Tbsp poppyseeds
- 1½ tsp fine sea salt
- ½ cup [110 g] unsalted butter, cut into 1-in [2.5-cm] cubes or grated
- ¼ cup [60 ml] cold whole milk

In a large mixing bowl, whisk together both flours, the Cheddar, 1 tsp of the ses-ame seeds, ½ tsp of the poppyseeds, and the salt. Using a pastry blender or clean hands, mix the butter into the flour mix-ture until a crumbly dough has formed. Make a well in the center of the dough and pour in the milk. Fold the dry ingredients into the wet until combined and a large ball has formed.

Mix together the remaining 2 Tbsp ses-ame seeds and 1 Tbsp poppyseeds in a wide shallow dish. Shape the dough into a cylinder 2 in [5 cm] in diameter, roll in the seed mixture to coat completely, and then wrap in wax paper, twisting the ends of the wax paper to seal. Transfer to the freezer and let freeze for at least 1 hour or up to 2 months.

Line a baking sheet with parchment paper and preheat the oven to 350°F [180°C].

Slice the dough into circles ⅛ in [4 mm] thick and transfer to the prepared baking sheet. Bake for 15 minutes or until golden around the edges, rotating the tray half-way through. Let cool completely before serving.

Store leftovers in an airtight container at room temperature for up to 5 days.

Marinated Feta with Sun-Dried Tomato, Thyme, and Garlic

Marinating cheese is an easy way to add new flavors to the standards you are used to. I love the pop of color that sun-dried tomatoes and thyme give this jar of marinated feta; however, feel free to play around with other herbs and flavor combinations. You can make this the same day you are serving it, or make it ahead to let the flavors meld together even more.

MAKES 1 PT [455 G]

6 sprigs fresh thyme

7 oz [200 g] feta

2 garlic cloves

4 sun-dried tomatoes, halved

8 peppercorns

About 1¼ cups [300 ml] olive oil (or enough to completely cover ingredients in the jar)

Layer the thyme, feta, garlic, sun-dried tomatoes, and peppercorns into a sterile and dry 1-pt [16-oz] Mason jar. Top with enough olive oil so that everything is completely submerged.

Seal and place in the refrigerator for at least 2 hours or up to 2 weeks.

Remove from refrigerator at least 20 minutes before serving, as the olive oil will thicken up when chilled.

Whole-Grain Ale Mustard

This tangy and spicy mustard pairs nicely with sweet fruit and savory cheeses. Keep the mustard spicy as is or add more honey at the end to sweeten it up to your liking. Don't skip soaking the seeds overnight in the vinegar mixture, as it helps mellow them out. Yellow mustard seeds are milder than brown, so feel free to use all yellow if you want a milder result or more brown to make it even spicier.

MAKES 2 CUPS [450 G]

½ cup [100 g] **yellow mustard seeds**

¼ cup [50 g] **brown mustard seeds**

½ cup [120 ml] **apple cider vinegar**

½ cup [120 ml] **pale ale beer**

1 Tbsp **lightly packed brown sugar**

⅓ cup [110 g] **honey + more as needed**

Salt

Combine yellow and brown mustard seeds, the cider vinegar, beer, and brown sugar in a small bowl or medium glass jar. Cover and refrigerate for 24 hours.

Transfer to a food processor and process until almost smooth, about 30 seconds. Add the honey and process for another 15 seconds. Taste and season with more honey or salt, if needed.

Serve right away or store in an airtight container in the refrigerator for up to 1 month.

Pistachio Herb Pesto

We use a lot of fresh herbs for garnish in this book, so this recipe is a perfect way to use up any leftovers.

MAKES 1 CUP [270 G]

3 cups [80 g] fresh herb leaves (such as basil, mint, sage, or parsley)

⅓ cup [50 g] pistachios

1 garlic clove

1 Tbsp freshly squeezed lemon juice

2 Tbsp grated Parmesan cheese

½ cup [120 ml] olive oil

Fine sea salt

Freshly ground black pepper

In a food processor, pulse the herb leaves, pistachios, garlic clove, lemon juice, and Parmesan five times or until everything is chopped into small pieces. With the food processor running, slowly pour in the olive oil and process until a thick pesto forms, about 15 seconds. Season with salt and pepper.

Serve right away or store in an airtight container in the refrigerator for up to 5 days. Bring to room temperature before serving, as the olive oil may solidify in the refrigerator.

Baked Camembert with Candied Cherries and Toasted Pecans

You can't go wrong with this sweet-and-savory baked cheese dish. Delicious on its own or served with a board, this gooey cheese takes less than 20 minutes to prepare. The brown sugar on top won't melt when baking, and instead will harden over the cheese, making it easy to cut into and top with the cherry mixture. If you have trouble finding Camembert, you can switch in Brie here, but vegetarians should note that it can be tricky to find a vegetarian Brie.

SERVES 8 AS AN APPETIZER

8-oz [230-g] wheel Camembert cheese

5 Tbsp [60 g] lightly packed brown sugar

1 cup [110 g] chopped pecans

½ cup [75 g] frozen sour cherries

1 tsp balsamic vinegar

Preheat the oven to 375°F [190°C] and line a large baking dish with parchment paper.

Place the cheese in the prepared baking dish and top with 2 Tbsp of the brown sugar. Bake for 7 minutes, and then add the pecans to the baking dish to toast. Bake for 5 minutes more, for a total of 12 minutes. Remove from the oven and let cool for 5 minutes.

In the meantime, add the remaining 3 Tbsp brown sugar, the sour cherries, and balsamic vinegar to a small saucepan over medium heat. Let cook until the brown sugar has completely dissolved, stirring often, and begins to simmer. Remove from the heat.

Add the baked cheese to a small serving bowl. Top with the cherry mixture and pecans and serve warm with crackers or crostini.

Candied Pistachios

These candied pistachios not only add an extra pop of color to any board or platter but also give a sweet and savory crunch that beautifully complements most cheeses and meats.

Before making this recipe, make sure you have a candy thermometer on hand and all your ingredients prepped; the coating hardens quickly, so you'll need to move fast once it's reached the right temperature. It can be hard to find shelled pistachios that haven't already been salted, so I compensated for that in the recipe by using salted pistachios instead of adding the salt into the baking process.

SERVES 6

1 cup [200 g] sugar

½ teaspoon ground cinnamon

¼ teaspoon cream of tartar

¼ cup [60 ml] water

1½ cups [180 g] shelled lightly salted pistachios

Line a baking sheet with parchment paper and set aside.

In a medium saucepan over medium heat, add the sugar, cinnamon, cream of tartar, and water. Bring to a boil and stir continuously, about 5 minutes. Once boiling, do not stir anymore and only swirl the mixture around from this point on. Using a candy thermometer, let the mixture boil until it reaches 240°F [116°C] (soft ball), gently swirling the mixture around every minute or so.

Once at 240°F [116°C], remove from the heat and quickly stir in the pistachios until they are completely coated.

Transfer the pistachios to the prepared baking sheet and spread into a single layer. Let cool completely and break apart, if any have stuck together, before serving.

Store in an airtight container at room temperature for up to 10 days.

Index

Acknowledgments

We want to start out by thanking you for picking up, reading, and cooking through our book.

Also, thank you so much to the team at Chronicle Books (Sarah Billingsley, Rachel Hiles, Alice Chau, Amy Cleary, and Alexandra Brown in particular) for bringing this book to life. And to our agent, Cindy Uh, for coming to us with this project and always having our backs.

Thank you to our families and friends for the endless support throughout the book-writing process. And extra thanks to Ryan Boyce and Susie Tanney—we never could have devoured all of the food ourselves.

Thank you to Oliver Winery in Bloomington, Indiana, for supplying the wine photographed in this book. We love collaborating with delicious local companies and are very thankful to have such a supportive winery so close to home.

Finally, thanks to our boxer pooch who was always willing to help Shelly clean up any food that dropped on the floor while recipe testing. And to Alanis Morissette for reissuing *Jagged Little Pill* on LP, which was on constant rotation while we photographed this book.

Chili Garlic Lime Compound Butter

MAKES ½ CUP [110 G] COMPOUND BUTTER

- **½ cup [110 g] unsalted butter at room temperature**
- **1 tsp chili garlic paste**
- **1 tsp fresh lime zest**
- **1½ tsp freshly squeezed lime juice (from about 1 lime)**
- **Dash of fine sea salt**

Combine the butter, chili garlic paste, lime zest and juice, and salt in a food processor and process until the butter is smooth and the ingredients are completely incorporated, about 20 seconds.

Transfer the compound butter to a dish to serve right away or roll it up in parchment paper and store it in the refrigerator for at least 3 hours, or until firm.

Serve within 5 days or store it in the freezer, in an airtight container, for up to 6 weeks.

Compound Butters Three Ways

Compound butter is just a fancy way to refer to flavored butters. These can be served soft, right out of the food processor, in a small dish, or rolled in parchment paper and firmed up in the refrigerator before being served by the slice. These butters have a great texture and color that will add depth to any presentation. They go great on fresh vegetables, crackers, or bread slices.

Blueberry Thyme Compound Butter

MAKES ½ CUP [110 G] COMPOUND BUTTER

- ½ cup [110 g] unsalted butter at room temperature
- 1½ Tbsp dried blueberries
- 1½ tsp fresh thyme
- 1½ tsp honey
- Dash of fine sea salt

Combine the butter, dried blueberries, thyme, honey, and salt in a food processor and process until the butter is smooth and the ingredients are completely incorporated, about 20 seconds.

Transfer the compound butter to a dish to serve right away or roll it up in parchment paper and store in the refrigerator for at least 3 hours, until firm.

Serve within 5 days or store it in the freezer, in an airtight container, for up to 6 weeks.

Vanilla Cinnamon Compound Butter

MAKES ½ CUP [110 G] COMPOUND BUTTER

- ½ cup [110 g] unsalted butter at room temperature
- 1½ tsp ground cinnamon
- Seeds from 1 vanilla bean
- 1½ tsp honey
- Dash of fine sea salt

Combine the butter, cinnamon, vanilla bean seeds, honey, and salt in a food processor and process until the butter is smooth and the ingredients are completely incorporated, about 20 seconds.

Transfer the compound butter to a dish to serve right away or roll it up in parchment paper and store in the refrigerator for at least 3 hours, until firm.

Serve within 5 days or store it in the freezer, in an airtight container, for up to 6 weeks.